STARTERS

by
Jean Paré

www.**company's**coming.com
visit our web-site

Dedication

Try this for starters!

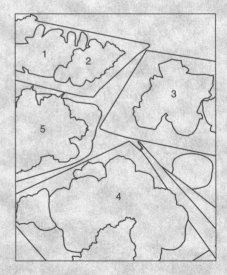

Cover Photo

Props Courtesy Of: Scona Clayworks
The Bay

STARTERS

Third Printing November 1999

Canadian Cataloguing in Publication Data

Paré, Jean
Company's Coming, Starters

Issued also in French under title: Les entrées
Includes index.
ISBN 1-895455-60-X

1.Appetizers. I. Title. II. Title: Starters.

TX740.P349 1999   641.8'12   C99-900934-6

Published and Distributed by
Company's Coming Publishing Limited
2311 - 96 Street
Edmonton, Alberta, Canada T6N 1G3
www.companyscoming.com

**Published Simultaneously in
Canada and the United States of America**

Printed In Canada

Company's Coming Cookbooks
by Jean Paré

COMPANY'S COMING SERIES

- 150 DELICIOUS SQUARES
- CASSEROLES
- MUFFINS & MORE
- SALADS
- APPETIZERS
- DESSERTS
- SOUPS & SANDWICHES
- HOLIDAY ENTERTAINING
- COOKIES
- VEGETABLES
- MAIN COURSES
- PASTA
- CAKES
- BARBECUES
- DINNERS OF THE WORLD
- LUNCHES
- PIES
- LIGHT RECIPES
- MICROWAVE COOKING
- PRESERVES
- LIGHT CASSEROLES
- CHICKEN, ETC.
- KIDS COOKING
- FISH & SEAFOOD
- BREADS
- MEATLESS COOKING
- COOKING FOR TWO
- BREAKFASTS & BRUNCHES
- SLOW COOKER RECIPES
- PIZZA!
- ONE-DISH MEALS
- STARTERS
- STIR-FRY ◀NEW▶ (March 2000)

SELECT SERIES

- SAUCES & MARINADES
- GROUND BEEF
- BEANS & RICE
- 30-MINUTE MEALS
- MAKE-AHEAD SALADS
- NO-BAKE DESSERTS

GREATEST HITS

- BISCUITS, MUFFINS & LOAVES
- DIPS, SPREADS & DRESSINGS
- SOUPS & SALADS ◀NEW▶ (April 2000)
- SANDWICHES & WRAPS ◀NEW▶ (April 2000)

ASSORTED TITLES

- COMPANY'S COMING FOR CHRISTMAS
- EASY ENTERTAINING
- MILLENNIUM EDITION

table of Contents

the Jean Paré story

Jean Paré grew up understanding that the combination of family, friends and home cooking is the essence of a good life. From her mother she learned to appreciate good cooking, while her father praised even her earliest attempts. When she left home she took with her many acquired family recipes, her love of cooking and her intriguing desire to read recipe books like novels!

In 1963, when her four children had all reached school age, Jean volunteered to cater to the 50th anniversary of the Vermilion School of Agriculture, now Lakeland College. Working out of her home, Jean prepared a dinner for over 1000 people which launched a flourishing catering operation that continued for over eighteen years. During that time she was provided with countless opportunities to test new ideas with immediate feedback—resulting in empty plates and contented customers! Whether preparing cocktail sandwiches for a house party or serving a hot meal for 1500 people, Jean Paré earned a reputation for good food, courteous service and reasonable prices.

"Why don't you write a cookbook?" Time and again, as requests for her recipes mounted, Jean was asked that question. Jean's response was to team up with her son, Grant Lovig, in the fall of 1980 to form Company's Coming Publishing Limited. April 14, 1981, marked the debut of "150 DELICIOUS SQUARES", the first Company's Coming cookbook in what soon would become Canada's most popular cookbook series.

Jean Paré's operation has grown steadily from the early days of working out of a spare bedroom in her home. Full-time staff includes marketing personnel located in major cities across Canada. Home Office is based in Edmonton, Alberta in a modern building constructed specially for the company.

Today the company distributes throughout Canada and the United States in addition to numerous overseas markets, all under the guidance of Jean's daughter, Gail Lovig. Best-sellers many times over, Company's Coming cookbooks are published in English and French, plus a Spanish-language edition is available in Mexico. Familiar and trusted in home kitchens the world over, Company's Coming cookbooks are offered in a variety of formats, including the original softcover series.

Jean Paré's approach to cooking has always called for quick and easy recipes using everyday ingredients. Even when travelling, she is constantly on the lookout for new ideas to share with her readers. At home, she can usually be found researching and writing recipes, or working in the company's test kitchen. Jean continues to gain new supporters by adhering to what she calls "the golden rule of cooking": never share a recipe you wouldn't use yourself. It's an approach that works—*millions of times over!*

Foreword

Starters are those morsels that we serve at the beginning of an evening of entertaining. They can be bite-size appetizers and finger foods, or a served soup or salad. They make a great start to any gathering and often help to get conversation going.

Appetizers and finger foods became fashionable in the early twentieth century. Since then, they have evolved into a multitude of morsels. With the explosion over the past one hundred years of canned and packaged ingredients, there is no end to what can be tucked inside phyllo pastry or stuffed into a mushroom cap.

Today's appetizers are fresh and varied, bright in colors, and even exotic in appearance. But they are all easy and most can be made ahead and frozen. What a welcome surprise for unexpected company to be served warm-from-the-oven Mushroom Pastries or Green Chili Bites—both from your freezer not 12 minutes earlier! Try to keep your serving sizes to one or two bites, and always serve with small plates or cocktail napkins. You may want to invest in decorative cocktail picks and small fancy spreaders.

Choose starters that have a variety of textures, colors and tastes. The ratio of hot to cold will depend on the time of year, the time of day and whether additional food will be offered. You don't want your appetizers to spoil dinner, but if you aren't serving a larger meal, you won't want your guests to go hungry.

Consider passing around only a few appetizers; then begin your meal with a starter soup or salad. The purpose of the starter is to stimulate the appetite for the meal to follow—not to compete with it. Starter soups and salads in this book are light and mellow in flavor and are meant to be served in smaller portions.

Cocktail parties, bridal showers, office gatherings, aprés-ski groups and even your volunteer-windup, are perfect opportunities for appetizers. Pass around a plate of hot Shrimp Kabobs, or have a platter of Beefy Roll-Ups and Chili Rolls handy for guests to serve themselves. Even Sushi and Dolmades can be assembled with relative ease for a trendy treat.

For a great beginning—choose STARTERS!

Jean Paré

Each recipe has been analyzed using the most updated version of the Canadian Nutrient File from Health And Welfare Canada which is based upon the United States Department of Agriculture (USDA) Nutrient Data Base.

Margaret Ng, B.Sc. (Hon), M.A.

Registered Dietician

PARMESAN TOAST

It doesn't get much easier than this.

Hard margarine (or butter), softened	½ cup	125 mL
Grated Parmesan cheese	¼ cup	60 mL
Baguette, cut into ½ inch (12 mm) slices	½	½

Mash margarine and cheese with fork on plate.

Arrange baguette slices on ungreased broiler tray. Broil to toast 1 side. Turn slices over. Spread 1 tbsp. (15 mL) cheese mixture on each slice. Broil until golden. Makes 12.

1 slice: 137 Calories; 9.4 g Total Fat; 245 mg Sodium; 3 g Protein; 11 g Carbohydrate; trace Dietary Fiber

CHEESY PARTY BREAD

This canapé has a good flavor served cold but it's even better when served warm.

Pork sausage meat	½ lb.	225 g
Lean ground beef	½ lb.	225 g
Process cheese loaf (such as Velveeta), cut up	½ lb.	225 g
Salt	¼ tsp.	1 mL
Pepper	⅛ tsp.	0.5 mL
Garlic powder	¼ tsp.	1 mL
Dried whole oregano	½ tsp.	2 mL
Cayenne pepper	⅛ tsp.	0.5 mL
Cocktail-size rye bread slices	32	32

Scramble-fry sausage meat and ground beef in frying pan until no longer pink. Drain.

Add next 6 ingredients. Stir until cheese is melted. Cool slightly. Makes 2 cups (500 mL) filling.

Arrange bread slices on ungreased baking sheet. Spread 1 tbsp. (15 mL) filling on each slice. (May be frozen at this point.) Bake in 350°F (175°C) oven for about 10 minutes. Makes 32.

1 canapé: 63 Calories; 3.4 g Total Fat; 218 mg Sodium; 4 g Protein; 4 g Carbohydrate; trace Dietary Fiber

Roasted pepper with cheese is a delight to eat.

Medium red pepper	1	1
Water	½ cup	125 mL
Cornstarch	1 tsp.	5 mL
Balsamic vinegar	¼ cup	60 mL
White vinegar	2 tbsp.	30 mL
Prepared mustard	1½ tbsp.	25 mL
Prepared horseradish	1 tsp.	5 mL
Cooking oil	1 tsp.	5 mL
Worcestershire sauce	¼ tsp.	1 mL
Cayenne pepper	⅛ tsp.	0.5 mL
Garlic powder (or 1 clove, minced)	¼ tsp.	1 mL
Part-skim mozzarella cheese, cut into **¼ inch (6 mm) cubes**	8 oz.	250 g
Chopped pitted ripe olives	¼ cup	60 mL
Baguette, cut into ½ inch (12 mm) slices	1	1

Set red pepper on ungreased pie plate. Bake in 350°F (175°C) oven for 15 minutes. Turn pepper. Bake for 15 to 20 minutes. Cool enough to handle. Peel, seed and dice. Turn into medium bowl.

Stir water and cornstarch together in small saucepan. Heat and stir until boiling and thickened. Remove from heat. Set aside.

Stir in next 8 ingredients. Add to red pepper. Cool.

Add cheese cubes and olives. Stir well. Cover. Marinate in refrigerator for several hours or overnight, stirring occasionally. Drain well. Makes 1⅔ cups (400 mL) topping.

Arrange baguette slices on ungreased broiler tray. Broil to toast top sides. Turn slices over. Using a slotted spoon, place 1 tbsp. (15 mL) cheese mixture on each slice. Broil until golden. Makes about 24.

1 slice: 86 Calories; 2.5 g Total Fat; 175 mg Sodium; 4 g Protein; 11 g Carbohydrate; trace Dietary Fiber

Pictured on page 89.

SHRIMP CURRY ON TOAST

Delicate curry flavor. Toast points always go quickly.

Cooking oil	2 tsp.	10 mL
Chopped onion	1/2 cup	125 mL
Chopped fresh mushrooms	1/2 cup	125 mL
Grated carrot	1/3 cup	75 mL
Garlic clove, minced (or 1/4 tsp., 1 mL, garlic powder)	1	1
Reserved liquid from shrimp		
Vegetable (or seafood) bouillon powder	1 tsp.	5 mL
Curry powder	1/2 tsp.	2 mL
Canned cocktail (or broken) shrimp, drained and rinsed, liquid reserved	4 oz.	113 g
Light cream cheese, softened	4 oz.	125 g
White (or whole wheat) sandwich bread slices, crusts removed	10	10
Medium coconut, sprinkle (optional)		

Heat cooking oil in frying pan. Add onion, mushrooms, carrot and garlic. Sauté until onion is soft.

Stir in reserved shrimp liquid, bouillon powder and curry powder. Cook until most of liquid is evaporated. Remove from heat.

Add shrimp and cream cheese. Mash together to make spreadable mixture. Makes 1 1/4 cups (300 mL) shrimp spread.

Toast 1 side of bread. Spread 2 tbsp. (30 mL) shrimp spread on untoasted side of each bread slice. Cut into Toast Points, page 14. Sprinkle with coconut. Arrange on ungreased baking sheet. Broil about 6 inches (15 cm) from heat until hot and coconut is toasted. Makes about 40.

1 toast point: 30 Calories; 1 g Total Fat; 81 mg Sodium; 2 g Protein; 4 g Carbohydrate; trace Dietary Fiber

Variation: Omit coconut. Broil then garnish with a bit of seafood sauce or mango chutney.

BACON CHEESE FILLING

Fill Toast Cups, page 14, or mini puff pastry patty shells, with about ½ tbsp. (7 mL) filling. Works great as a spread too. Lots of bacon flavor. Chives add a zestiness.

Bacon slices	4	4
Light cream cheese, softened	4 oz.	125 g
Milk	1½ tbsp.	25 mL
Dried chopped chives (or green onion)	1 tbsp.	15 mL

Cook bacon in frying pan until crisp. Drain. Cool. Crumble or chop.

Mash cream cheese and milk together well in small bowl. Mix in bacon and chives. Makes ⅔ cup (150 mL).

½ tbsp. (7 mL): 17 Calories; 1.4 g Total Fat; 68 mg Sodium; 1 g Protein; trace Carbohydrate; 0 g Dietary Fiber

HAM PINWHEELS

Make one day ahead or make and freeze ahead.

Canned ham flakes	6½ oz.	184 g
Salad dressing (or mayonnaise)	3 tbsp.	50 mL
Worcestershire sauce	1 tbsp.	15 mL
Prepared mustard	1 tsp.	5 mL
Onion powder	¼ tsp.	1 mL
Day-old unsliced white (or whole wheat) bread loaf, sliced lengthwise (at bakery)	1	1
Hard margarine (or butter), softened	¼ cup	60 mL
Gherkins, approximately	9	9

Mash first 5 ingredients together with fork in small bowl.

Remove crusts from 3 long slices of bread. Roll each slice with rolling pin to flatten slightly. Thinly spread each slice with margarine to edge. Spread with ham mixture to edge. Place gherkins, end to end, along short edge of each slice. Roll up. Place seam side down in container. Cover with damp tea towel. Chill. Slice thinly to serve. Cuts into 12 pinwheel slices per roll, for a total of 36.

1 pinwheel: 65 Calories; 3.3 g Total Fat; 185 mg Sodium; 2 g Protein; 7 g Carbohydrate; trace Dietary Fiber

CRAB PUFFS

Tasty and colorful. Freezing is not recommended.

Salad dressing (or mayonnaise)	2 tbsp.	30 mL
Milk	3 tbsp.	50 mL
Prepared mustard	1 tsp.	5 mL
Hot pepper sauce	⅛ tsp.	0.5 mL
Lemon juice	1 tsp.	5 mL
Parsley flakes	½ tsp.	2 mL
Onion powder	¼ tsp.	1 mL
Salt	¼ tsp.	1 mL
Chopped pimiento	1 tbsp.	15 mL
Canned crabmeat, drained and cartilage removed	4¼ oz.	120 g
All-purpose flour	1 tsp.	5 mL
Egg whites (large), room temperature	3	3
White (or whole wheat) sandwich bread slices, crusts removed	12	12
Grated part-skim mozzarella cheese	¾ cup	175 mL
Pimiento strips (or pimiento-stuffed green olive slices)	48	48

Stir first 11 ingredients in medium bowl in order given.

Beat egg whites in small bowl until stiff. Fold into crab mixture.

Arrange bread slices on ungreased baking sheet. Spread about 2 tbsp. (30 mL) crab mixture over each slice. Sprinkle with cheese. Top with pimiento strip placed down center of each side of crab mixture. Bake in 350°F (175°C) oven for 15 to 20 minutes until puffed and golden. Cut each slice into Toast Triangles, page 14. Makes 48.

1 toast triangle: 37 Calories; 1.3 g Total Fat; 95 mg Sodium; 2 g Protein; 5 g Carbohydrate; trace Dietary Fiber

ONION TOAST POINTS

Broils to an orange shade. Tangy.

Salad dressing (or mayonnaise)	½ cup	125 mL
Finely chopped red onion	½ cup	125 mL
Paprika	1 tsp.	5 mL
Cayenne pepper	⅛ tsp.	0.5 mL
Salt	⅛ tsp.	0.5 mL
Pepper, just a pinch		

(continued on next page)

| White (or whole wheat) sandwich bread slices, crusts removed | 6 | 6 |

Stir first 6 ingredients in small bowl. Makes 1 cup (250 mL).

Arrange bread slices on ungreased broiler tray. Broil to toast on 1 side only. Turn over. Spread untoasted sides of slices with about 2½ tbsp. (37 mL) onion mixture. Broil about 6 inches (15 cm) from heat for about 4 minutes until bubbly hot. Watch closely. Cut into Toast Points, page 14. Makes 24.

1 toast point: 44 Calories; 2.7 g Total Fat; 79 mg Sodium; 1 g Protein; 4 g Carbohydrate; trace Dietary Fiber

TENDERLOIN ON TOAST

A make-ahead sure-to-be-a-hit canapé.

Soy sauce	3 tbsp.	50 mL
Ketchup	3 tbsp.	50 mL
Brown sugar, packed	3 tbsp.	50 mL
Sherry (or alcohol-free sherry)	3 tbsp.	50 mL
Red food coloring	1 tsp.	5 mL
Pork tenderloin	1 lb.	454 g
Toast Rounds, page 14	24	24
Hard margarine (or butter), softened	2 tbsp.	30 mL

Mix first 5 ingredients in small bowl. Pour into sealable plastic bag.

Place tenderloin in bag. Seal. Marinate in refrigerator all day or overnight, turning bag occasionally. Remove pork from marinade. Place in ungreased 8 or 9 inch (20 or 22 cm) square pan. Cook, uncovered, in 375°F (190°C) oven for 20 minutes. Brush with marinade. Cook for 10 to 20 minutes until cooked. Chill. Slice into ⅛ inch (3 mm) slices.

Spread margarine on 1 side of each Toast Round. Serve slice of tenderloin on buttered side. Makes 96.

1 canapé: 23 Calories; 0.5 g Total Fat; 71 mg Sodium; 1 g Protein; 3 g Carbohydrate; trace Dietary Fiber

TOAST CUPS

Quick-and-easy containers for spreads or a mousse.

White (or whole wheat) sandwich bread 9   9
slices, crusts removed

Cut each bread slice into 4 squares. Press into ungreased muffin cups. Bake on bottom rack in 350°F (175°C) oven for about 15 minutes until browned. Cool. Store in plastic bag or other container. Fill before serving, or let guests help themselves. Makes 36.

1 toast cup: 17 Calories; 0.2 g Total Fat; 32 mg Sodium; 1 g Protein; 3 g Carbohydrate; trace Dietary Fiber

Variation: Lightly butter both sides of bread before pressing into muffin cups. Bread may also be cut into 2½ inch (6.4 cm) circles, both sides buttered, and pressed into cups. Bake as above.

TOAST POINTS: Arrange uncut bread slices on ungreased broiler tray. Broil 1 side only until lightly browned. ❶ Cut each slice down the center to make 2 rectangles. Cut each rectangle cornerwise to make 4 elongated triangles.

TOAST SQUARES: Arrange uncut bread slices on ungreased broiler tray. Broil 1 side only until lightly browned. ❷ Cut each slice into 4 squares rather than elongated triangles.

TOAST TRIANGLES: Arrange uncut bread slices on ungreased broiler tray. Broil 1 side only until lightly browned. ❸ Cut each slice into 4 even triangles, cutting diagonally from corner to corner.

TOAST ROUNDS: Slice small loaf, such as submarine bun or baguette, into round slices. Broil 1 side, or leave plain.

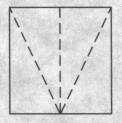 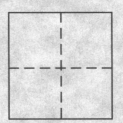 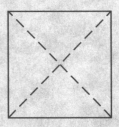

❶ Toast Points   ❷ Toast Squares   ❸ Toast Triangles

SEAFOOD SQUARES

These can be made ahead. Cover to reheat.

Biscuit mix	2 cups	500 mL
Milk	½ cup	125 mL
Onion powder	¼ tsp.	1 mL
Grated medium or sharp Cheddar cheese	1 cup	250 mL
Grated Monterey Jack cheese	1 cup	250 mL
Canned broken shrimp, drained and rinsed	2 × 4 oz.	2 × 113 g
Canned crabmeat, drained and cartilage removed	5 oz.	142 g
Large eggs	6	6
Light cream (half-and-half)	2 cups	500 mL
Salt	½ tsp.	2 mL
Pepper	¼ tsp.	1 mL

Stir biscuit mix, milk and onion powder together in medium bowl to form a soft ball. Press in bottom of ungreased 9 x 13 inch (22 x 33 cm) pan. Bake in 375°F (190°C) oven for 15 minutes to partially cook.

Sprinkle crust with both cheeses, shrimp and crabmeat.

Beat eggs in medium bowl until frothy. Add cream, salt and pepper. Mix. Pour over top of seafood. Bake for about 35 minutes until knife inserted in center comes out clean. Let stand for 5 to 10 minutes. Cut into squares. Makes 54.

1 square: 65 Calories; 3.7 g Total Fat; 151 mg Sodium; 4 g Protein; 4 g Carbohydrate; trace Dietary Fiber

Paré Pointer

All leaping lettuce is found in a tossed salad.

SHRIMP SQUARES

Serve as a finger food or as a first course starter.

White (or whole wheat) sandwich bread slices, crusts removed	6	6
Hard margarine (or butter), softened	2 tbsp.	30 mL
Canned small shrimp, drained and rinsed	4 oz.	113 g
Grated medium Cheddar cheese	½ cup	125 mL
Mayonnaise (not salad dressing)	2 tbsp.	30 mL
Parsley flakes	1 tsp.	5 mL
Worcestershire sauce	¼ tsp.	1 mL
Onion salt	¼ tsp.	1 mL
Paprika, sprinkle		

Arrange bread slices on ungreased broiler tray. Lightly butter 1 side of each slice. Cut each slice into 4 smaller squares. Broil buttered sides until lightly browned. Turn over. Set aside.

Mash shrimp, cheese and mayonnaise together in medium bowl, adding more mayonnaise if too dry. Mix in parsley, Worcestershire sauce and onion salt. Spread unbuttered side of each toast square with 1½ tsp. (7 mL) shrimp mixture.

Sprinkle with paprika. Broil until sizzling hot. Serve. Makes 24 small squares, or serves 6 as a first course appetizer.

1 square: 49 Calories; 3 g Total Fat; 87 mg Sodium; 2 g Protein; 3 g Carbohydrate; trace Dietary Fiber

CRAB SQUARES: Use crabmeat instead of shrimp.

1. Wiener Wisps, page 73
2. Spinach Dip 'N' Bowl, page 31
3. Snackin' Potato Skins (Variations), page 79
4. Toads, page 23
5. Stuffed Mushrooms, page 78
6. Southern Pizza, page 22
7. Chicken Pizza, page 20
8. Beefy Roll-Ups, page 94

Props Courtesy Of: Clays Handmade Tile & Ceramic
Le Gnome

An attractive twist to the usual bruschetta. Colorful with flavor to match.

BASIC PIZZA CRUST

All-purpose flour	1½ cups	375 mL
Instant yeast	1¼ tsp.	6 mL
Salt	¼ tsp.	1 mL
Cooking oil	2 tbsp.	30 mL
Very warm water	½ cup	125 mL

TOPPING

Salad dressing (or mayonnaise)	½ cup	125 mL
Grated Parmesan cheese	¼ cup	60 mL
Dried whole oregano	1 tsp.	5 mL
Dried sweet basil	½ tsp.	2 mL
Pepper	½ tsp.	2 mL
Garlic cloves, minced (or ½ tsp., 2 mL, garlic powder), optional	2	2
Chopped pitted ripe olives	⅓ cup	75 mL
Plum tomatoes, seeded and diced	3	3
Grated part-skim mozzarella cheese	1½ cups	375 mL

Basic Pizza Crust: Put flour, yeast and salt into food processor fitted with dough blade.

With machine running, pour cooking oil and warm water through feed tube. Process for about 30 seconds. Let dough rest, covered, for 15 minutes. Roll out on lightly floured surface. Press in greased 12 inch (30 cm) pizza pan or 9 x 13 inch (22 x 33 cm) pan. Poke holes all over crust, except edge, with fork. Bake on bottom rack in 425°F (220°C) oven for 8 minutes. Press down any bulges. Cool slightly.

Topping: Mix first 6 ingredients well in medium bowl. Spread over crust.

Sprinkle with olives, tomato and mozzarella cheese. Bake for about 8 minutes. Cuts into 16 long thin appetizer wedges or 24 squares.

1 wedge: 144 Calories; 8.3 g Total Fat; 193 mg Sodium; 5 g Protein; 12 g Carbohydrate; 1 g Dietary Fiber

Pictured on page 89.

CHICKEN PIZZA

Guests will love to fill their plates with these small wedges.

SWEET BISCUIT PIZZA CRUST

All-purpose flour	2 cups	500 mL
Baking powder	1 tbsp.	15 mL
Granulated sugar	1 tsp.	5 mL
Salt	1/4 tsp.	1 mL
Milk	2/3 cup	150 mL
Cooking oil	1 tbsp.	15 mL

TOPPING

Cooking oil	2 tsp.	10 mL
Boneless, skinless chicken breast halves (about 1/2 lb., 225 g), cut into very small dice	2	2
Chopped onion	3/4 cup	175 mL
Chopped green pepper	1/3 cup	75 mL
Garlic powder	1/8 tsp.	0.5 mL
Chili powder	1/8 tsp.	0.5 mL
Ground thyme	1/8 tsp.	0.5 mL
Cayenne pepper	1/8 tsp.	0.5 mL
Salt	1 tsp.	5 mL
Pepper	1/8 tsp.	0.5 mL
Picante salsa	6 tbsp.	100 mL
Grated part-skim mozzarella cheese	1 1/2 cups	375 mL

Sweet Biscuit Pizza Crust: Combine first 4 ingredients in medium bowl.

Add milk and cooking oil. Stir to form a soft ball. Turn out onto lightly floured surface. Knead 8 times. Divide into 4 equal portions. Roll out each portion into 7 inch (18 cm) diameter circle. Place on large greased baking sheet. Bake in 425°F (220°C) oven for 8 minutes to partially cook.

Topping: Heat cooking oil in frying pan. Add chicken, onion and green pepper. Scramble-fry until chicken is no longer pink and onion is golden.

Stir in next 6 ingredients.

(continued on next page)

Spread ¼ of salsa over each crust. Scatter ¼ of chicken mixture over salsa. Sprinkle each with ¼ of cheese. Bake for 6 minutes until hot and cheese is melted. Cut each pizza into 8 wedges. Makes 32 wedges.

1 wedge: 66 Calories; 1.9 g Total Fat; 186 mg Sodium; 4 g Protein; 8 g Carbohydrate; trace Dietary Fiber

Pictured on page 17.

Note: To make without partially baking crust, put topping onto unbaked crust. Bake on bottom rack in 450°F (230°C) oven for 10 minutes.

CHEESE TOASTIES

Be prepared to make lots. A popular flavor.

Grated sharp Cheddar cheese	1 cup	250 mL
Grated onion	2 tsp.	10 mL
Worcestershire sauce	¼ tsp.	1 mL
Lemon juice	1½ tsp.	7 mL
Cayenne pepper	¹⁄₁₆ tsp.	0.5 mL
Salt	¼ tsp.	1 mL
White (or whole wheat) sandwich bread slices, with crusts	8	8
Hard margarine (or butter), softened	3 tbsp.	50 mL

Mix first 6 ingredients well in small bowl.

Lay 4 bread slices on working surface. Divide cheese mixture among slices. Spread. Cover with remaining 4 slices. Spread tops with margarine. Turn over. Spread again with margarine. Cut off crusts. Cut each sandwich into 4 squares. Place all 16 squares in hot frying pan. Brown each side. Serve. Makes 16.

1 toastie: 84 Calories; 5.1 g Total Fat; 179 mg Sodium; 3 g Protein; 7 g Carbohydrate; trace Dietary Fiber

Paré Pointer

When tires get old there is nothing left to do but retire them.

SOUTHERN PIZZA

Little bit of corn and chili powder on a biscuit crust. A bit of the South.

BISCUIT PIZZA CRUST

All-purpose flour	2 cups	500 mL
Baking powder	1 tbsp.	15 mL
Salt	¼ tsp.	1 mL
Water	⅔ cup	150 mL
Cooking oil	1 tbsp.	15 mL

TOPPING

Cooking oil	2 tsp.	10 mL
Lean ground beef	½ lb.	225 g
Chopped onion	½ cup	125 mL
Chopped green pepper	¼ cup	60 mL
Canned tomatoes, drained, chopped and drained again	14 oz.	398 mL
Frozen kernel corn	½ cup	125 mL
Chili powder	1 tsp.	5 mL
Dried whole oregano	½ tsp.	2 mL
Garlic powder	¼ tsp.	1 mL
Dried sweet basil	¼ tsp.	1 mL
Salt	½ tsp.	2 mL
Pepper	⅛ tsp.	0.5 mL
Grated part-skim mozzarella cheese	1⅓ cups	325 mL

Biscuit Pizza Crust: Measure flour, baking powder and salt into medium bowl. Stir.

Add water and cooking oil. Mix into soft ball. Turn out onto lightly floured surface. Knead 8 times. Divide and roll into 4 circles, 7 inches (18 cm) in diameter. Place on greased baking sheets.

Topping: Heat cooking oil in frying pan. Add ground beef, onion and green pepper. Scramble-fry until beef is no longer pink and onion and pepper are soft and golden. Drain.

Stir next 8 ingredients together in medium bowl. Spread ¼ of corn mixture over each crust. Spoon ¼ of meat mixture over corn mixture.

(continued on next page)

Sprinkle each pizza with ¼ of cheese. Bake on bottom rack in 425°F (220°C) oven for about 15 minutes. Cut each pizza into 8 wedges, for a total of 32.

1 wedge: 64 Calories; 2 g Total Fat; 113 mg Sodium; 4 g Protein; 8 g Carbohydrate; 1 g Dietary Fiber

Pictured on page 17.

Pictured on page 17.

TOADS

Serve hot from the oven or reheat later.

Cooking oil	1 tsp.	5 mL
Cocktail-size sausages (or small sausages, halved)	12	12
All-purpose flour	1 cup	250 mL
Salt	¼ tsp.	1 mL
Large egg	1	1
Milk	1¼ cups	300 mL
Cooking oil	2 tbsp.	30 mL

Heat first amount of cooking oil in frying pan. Add sausages. Brown.

Place flour, salt, egg and milk in small bowl. Beat until smooth.

Put ½ tsp. (2 mL) second amount of cooking oil and 1 small browned sausage into each muffin cup. Heat in 425°F (220°C) oven for 5 minutes. Pour milk mixture quickly over each sausage. Bake for 20 minutes until risen and golden brown. Makes 12.

1 toad: 126 Calories; 7.5 g Total Fat; 227 mg Sodium; 4 g Protein; 10 g Carbohydrate; trace Dietary Fiber

Pictured on page 17.

Pictured on page 17.

Paré Pointer

She was enjoying the spring flowers until she heard the cro-cuss.

SHRIMP CANAPÉS

Looks pretty on the darkest bread you can find.

SHRIMP FILLING

Canned shrimp, drained and rinsed	4 oz.	113 g
Salad dressing (or mayonnaise)	3 tbsp.	50 mL
Ketchup	1½ tbsp.	25 mL
Prepared horseradish	¼ tsp.	1 mL
Cocktail-size dark (such as pumpernickel) bread slices	20	20
Pimiento strips, for garnish		

Shrimp Filling: Mash first 4 ingredients together in small bowl. Makes ⅞ cup (200 mL) filling.

Cut bread slices into rounds with 1¾ inch (4.5 cm) cookie cutter. Spoon or pipe shrimp mixture over top of each slice. Garnish with pimiento. Makes 20.

1 canapé: 34 Calories; 1.3 g Total Fat; 75 mg Sodium; 2 g Protein; 4 g Carbohydrate; trace Dietary Fiber

HAMWICHES

A very moist filling that can be used in Mini Cream Puff Shells, page 88.

HAM FILLING

Canned ham flakes, with liquid	6½ oz.	184 g
Salad dressing (or mayonnaise)	1½ tbsp.	25 mL
Sweet pickle relish	1 tbsp.	15 mL
Dried chives	2 tsp.	10 mL
Pumpernickel bread slices	6	6
Hard margarine (or butter), softened	2 tbsp.	30 mL

Ham Filling: Break up ham with liquid in small bowl. Add salad dressing, relish and chives. Mash together well. Makes ¾ cup (175 mL) filling.

Make sandwiches with 3 pieces of bread and 2 layers of filling, buttering bread on both sides of filling. Cut off crusts. Cut into four 1 inch (2.5 cm) slices. Lay slices flat. Cut into thirds. Serve sandwiches on their sides. Makes 24.

1 hamwich: 48 Calories; 3 g Total Fat; 160 mg Sodium; 2 g Protein; 4 g Carbohydrate; trace Dietary Fiber

EGG RIBBONS

These eye-appealing little sandwiches are enjoyed by all.

Large hard-boiled eggs, chopped	6	6
Finely diced celery	¼ cup	60 mL
Salad dressing (or mayonnaise)	¼ cup	60 mL
Sweet pickle relish	2 tbsp.	30 mL
Onion powder	¼ tsp.	1 mL
Salt	½ tsp.	2 mL
Day-old dark bread slices	8	8
Day-old white bread slices	4	4
Hard margarine (or butter), softened	¼ cup	60 mL

Mix first 6 ingredients in small bowl.

Use 2 dark bread slices and 1 white bread slice per stack. Lightly butter 1 side of each dark slice. Spread with ⅛ of egg mixture. Lightly butter both sides of white slice. Place on top of egg mixture. Spread top side with ⅛ of egg mixture. Place remaining dark slice, buttered side down, on top of egg mixture. Repeat with remaining 6 dark slices and 3 white slices, to make a total of 4 stacks. Cut off crusts. Wrap each stack. Chill. To serve, cut into ½ inch (12 mm) layered slices. Cut each slice into 3 or 4 finger sandwiches. Makes about 48.

1 sandwich: 42 Calories; 2.5 g Total Fat; 92 mg Sodium; 1 g Protein; 4 g Carbohydrate; trace Dietary Fiber

SESAME ROUNDS

Serve these hot or cold.

White (or whole wheat or pumpernickel) bread slices	12	12
Hard margarine (or butter), softened	½ cup	125 mL
Toasted sesame seeds	⅓ cup	75 mL

Cut 4 rounds per slice of bread, using 1¾ inch (4.5 cm) cookie cutter. Generously butter 1 side of each round to edge. Press buttered side into sesame seeds to coat. Arrange, seed side up, on greased baking sheet. Bake in 350°F (175°C) oven for about 15 minutes until browned. Makes 48.

1 round: 41 Calories; 2.8 g Total Fat; 56 mg Sodium; 1 g Protein; 3 g Carbohydrate; trace Dietary Fiber

Pictured on page 107.

HOT BREAD PUFFS

Cheese-coated cubes are bites of bliss. Recipe may easily be halved.

Day-old unsliced white (or whole wheat) bread loaf, crust removed	1	1
Hard margarine (or butter)	1 cup	250 mL
Cream cheese	8 oz.	250 g
Grated sharp Cheddar cheese	3 cups	750 mL
Worcestershire sauce	2 tsp.	10 mL
Egg whites (large), room temperature	4	4

Cut bread loaf into 1 inch (2.5 cm) cubes. Place in freezer for about 30 minutes until partially frozen.

Combine next 4 ingredients in top of double boiler over simmering water. Stir often as mixture melts. Remove from heat.

Beat egg whites in small bowl until stiff. Fold into hot mixture until no streaks appear. Pierce partially frozen bread cubes with fork. Dip into hot mixture to coat. Transfer to ungreased baking sheet. Chill all day or overnight. Just before serving, bake in 400°F (205°C) oven for about 10 minutes until lightly browned. To keep on hand, freeze on tray. Store in plastic container or bag. Thaw before baking. Makes about 120.

1 bread puff: 43 Calories; 3.4 g Total Fat; 64 mg Sodium; 1 g Protein; 2 g Carbohydrate; trace Dietary Fiber

SAUSAGE BREAD ROLLS

A very different sausage roll. Encased in bread and cheese. Quick to prepare.

Link sausages (about ½ lb., 225 g)	8	8
Hard margarine (or butter), softened	¼ cup	60 mL
Grated medium Cheddar cheese	1 cup	250 mL
White (or whole wheat) sandwich bread slices, crusts removed	8	8

Poke holes in sausages with tip of paring knife so fat can drain out. Cook sausages in frying pan. Drain. Cool.

Cream margarine and cheese together in small bowl.

(continued on next page)

Roll each bread slice flat with rolling pin. Spread both sides of each slice with cheese mixture using about 1 tbsp. (15 mL) per side. Place sausage on 1 edge. Roll up snugly like jelly roll. Repeat. Arrange on greased baking sheet. Bake in 375°F (190°C) oven for about 12 minutes until very hot. Cut each sausage roll into 3 pieces to serve. Makes 24.

1 piece: 78 Calories; 5.6 g Total Fat; 133 mg Sodium; 3 g Protein; 4 g Carbohydrate; trace Dietary Fiber

GRILLED CHEESE BITES

Guests will love these tiny sandwiches.

White (or whole wheat) sandwich bread slices, crusts removed	3	3
Pepper Monterey Jack cheese, sliced	3 oz.	85 g
White (or whole wheat) sandwich bread slices, crusts removed	3	3
Jalapeño pepper jelly	3 tbsp.	50 mL
Medium Cheddar cheese, thinly sliced	3 oz.	85 g
White (or whole wheat) sandwich bread slices, crusts removed	3	3
Large eggs, fork-beaten	2	2
Water	¼ cup	60 mL

Lay 3 bread slices on working surface. Divide Monterey Jack cheese slices on top of each slice. Set second bread slice over each. Spread each with 1 tbsp. (15 mL) jalapeño jelly. Layer Cheddar cheese slices over jelly followed by third bread slice. Cut each stack into 4 squares.

Mix egg and water in small bowl. Dip top and bottom of each small sandwich into egg mixture. Grill in hot well-greased frying pan, browning both sides. These can be made ahead, frozen in single layer on tray and stored in container in freezer. They are good thawed and eaten cold, or thaw and heat in 350°F (175°C) oven for about 5 minutes. Makes 12.

1 bite: 127 Calories; 5.9 g Total Fat; 197 mg Sodium; 6 g Protein; 12 g Carbohydrate; trace Dietary Fiber

BEEF BUNS

You can choose either small appetizer-size or larger lunch-size buns.

Beef stew meat, cut into ¾ inch (2 cm) cubes	**1½ lbs.**	**680 g**
Water, to cover		
Salt	**1 tsp.**	**5 mL**
Pepper	**½ tsp.**	**2 mL**
Cooking oil	**2 tsp.**	**10 mL**
Medium onion, chopped	**1**	**1**
Shredded cabbage, packed	**⅔ cup**	**150 mL**
Grated gingerroot	**1-2 tbsp.**	**15-30 mL**
Soy sauce	**¼ cup**	**60 mL**
Finely chopped green onion	**¼ cup**	**60 mL**
Brown sugar, packed	**2 tbsp.**	**30 mL**
Salt	**½ tsp.**	**2 mL**
Dried crushed chilies	**½ tsp.**	**2 mL**
Garlic powder	**¼ tsp.**	**1 mL**
Cornstarch	**2 tsp.**	**10 mL**
Liquid gravy browner	**2 tsp.**	**10 mL**
Frozen dinner roll dough, thawed (see Note)	**30**	**30**
Large egg, fork-beaten	**1**	**1**
Sesame seeds (not toasted)	**1 tbsp.**	**15 mL**

Boil stew meat, water and first amount of salt gently in large saucepan for at least 1½ hours until very tender. Strain and reserve ⅔ cup (150 mL) liquid. Cool meat. Process in food processor until shredded.

Heat cooking oil in large frying pan. Add onion. Sauté until soft.

Add cabbage and gingerroot. Sauté until cabbage is soft.

Stir in next 6 ingredients.

Mix reserved liquid, cornstarch and gravy browner in small cup. Stir into cabbage mixture until boiling and thickened. Add shredded meat. Stir. Cool. Makes about 3½ cups (875 mL) filling.

(continued on next page)

Divide buns in half. Roll each half into 2½ inch (6.4 cm) circle. Place 1 scant tbsp. (15 mL) beef filling in center. Moisten edge with water. Gather edge up to top, pinching to seal. Place seam side down, 1 inch (2.5 cm) apart, on 2 greased 11 × 17 inch (28 × 43 cm) baking sheets. Cover each with damp tea towel. Let stand in oven with light on and door closed for about 40 minutes until buns are doubled in size.

Brush buns with egg. Sprinkle with sesame seeds. Bake in 375°F (190°C) oven for about 15 minutes until lightly browned. Makes 60.

1 small bun: 102 Calories; 2.7 g Total Fat; 290 mg Sodium; 5 g Protein; 14 g Carbohydrate; 1 g Dietary Fiber

Pictured on page 125.

Note: For larger buns, roll whole bun into 4 inch (10 cm) circle. Spoon about 1½ tbsp. (25 mL) beef filling in center. Bake for about 20 minutes. Makes 30.

TUNA TOWERS

The unusual addition of grated apple gives this its good flavor. Contrasting colors of bread and filling make this very attractive.

TUNA FILLING

Canned flaked tuna, drained	6½ oz.	184 g
Grated peeled apple	⅓ cup	75 mL
Finely chopped celery	¼ cup	60 mL
Sweet pickle relish	1 tsp.	5 mL
Onion powder	¼ tsp.	1 mL
Salad dressing (or mayonnaise)	¼ cup	60 mL
Salt	⅛ tsp.	0.5 mL
Cocktail-size dark (such as pumpernickel) bread slices	60	60
Hard margarine (or butter), softened	3 tbsp.	50 mL
Pimiento-stuffed green olive slices, for garnish		

Tuna Filling: Combine first 7 ingredients in medium bowl. Stir together. Makes 1⅓ cups (325 mL) filling.

Cut out 1½ inch (3.8 cm) circles from each bread slice. Spread margarine and 1½ tsp. (7 mL) filling on each of 2 slices. Top with third slice. Repeat with remaining filling and bread slices. Garnish with olive slices. Makes 20.

1 tiered sandwich: 91 Calories; 3.7 g Total Fat; 200 mg Sodium; 4 g Protein; 11 g Carbohydrate; 1 g Dietary Fiber

STUFFING BALLS

What an aroma and with flavor to match!

Chopped onion	¼ cup	60 mL
Chopped celery	¼ cup	60 mL
Hard margarine (or butter)	2 tbsp.	30 mL
Canned cream-style corn	¾ cup	175 mL
Water	¼ cup	60 mL
Parsley flakes	1 tsp.	5 mL
Poultry seasoning	1 tsp.	5 mL
Salt	½ tsp.	2 mL
Pepper	⅛ tsp.	0.5 mL
Large eggs, fork-beaten	2	2
Fine dry bread crumbs	2 cups	500 mL
Thin bacon slices (about 1½ lbs., 680 g)	20	20

Sauté onion and celery in margarine in small frying pan until soft.

Combine corn, water, parsley flakes, poultry seasoning, salt, and pepper in large bowl. Stir in eggs. Add onion and celery mixture.

Add bread crumbs. Mix well. Chill for 30 minutes. Shape into 1 inch (2.5 cm) balls.

Cut bacon slices in half. Wrap each ball with bacon. Secure with wooden pick. To serve, place on ungreased baking sheet. Bake in 400°F (205°C) oven for 10 minutes. Drain. Turn. Bake for 10 minutes until bacon is cooked and browned. Drain on paper towel. Makes about 40.

4 stuffing balls: 54 Calories; 2.7 g Total Fat; 152 mg Sodium; 2 g Protein; 5 g Carbohydrate; trace Dietary Fiber

Paré Pointer

Better quit preening or you'll end up like a duck—down in the mouth.

SAVORY CURRY DIP

Curry flavor is middle of the road. Add as much as you like. Serve with fresh vegetables.

Salad dressing (or mayonnaise)	1 cup	250 mL
Onion flakes	1 tbsp.	15 mL
Prepared horseradish	2 tsp.	10 mL
Curry powder	1 tsp.	5 mL
Salt	1 tsp.	5 mL
Milk	½ cup	125 mL

Mix all 6 ingredients in small bowl. Makes 1⅓ cups (325 mL).

1 tbsp. (15 mL): 59 Calories; 5.6 g Total Fat; 196 mg Sodium; trace Protein; 2 g Carbohydrate; trace Dietary Fiber

SPINACH DIP 'N' BOWL

This makes a large amount, but don't be concerned, you make the dish to serve it in too! Serve surrounded with vegetables, bread chunks and crackers.

Frozen chopped spinach, thawed and squeezed dry	10 oz.	300 g
Salad dressing (or mayonnaise)	1 cup	250 mL
Sour cream	1 cup	250 mL
Chopped onion	½ cup	125 mL
Envelope dry vegetable soup mix	1 × 1½ oz.	1 × 45 g
Canned chopped water chestnuts, drained	10 oz.	284 mL
Round bread loaf, hollowed out	1	1

Place first 4 ingredients in blender. Process until smooth. Turn into medium bowl.

Stir in vegetable soup mix and water chestnuts. Cover. Chill for at least 2 hours. Makes 3¾ cups (925 mL).

Fill bread loaf with dip. Serve at room temperature or wrap in foil and heat in 300°F (150°C) oven for 2 to 3 hours.

2 tbsp. (30 mL) dip only: 63 Calories; 5.4 g Total Fat; 132 mg Sodium; 1 g Protein; 3 g Carbohydrate; trace Dietary Fiber

Pictured on page 17.

GUACAMOLE

Spiced just right. Green in color with tomato showing through. Serve with corn chips, tortilla chips or raw vegetables.

Medium avocados, peeled and mashed	2	2
Lime (or lemon) juice	3 tbsp.	50 mL
Finely chopped white (or red) onion	2 tbsp.	30 mL
Medium tomato, seeded and diced	1	1
Chili powder	1 tsp.	5 mL
Garlic powder	1/4 tsp.	1 mL
Cayenne pepper	1/4 tsp.	1 mL
Salt	1 tsp.	5 mL
Pepper	1/4 tsp.	1 mL

Mix all 9 ingredients in medium bowl. Makes 1³/₄ cups (425 mL).

1 tbsp. (15 mL): *24 Calories; 2.1 g Total Fat; 96 mg Sodium; trace Protein; 2 g Carbohydrate; trace Dietary Fiber*

Pictured on page 35.

CHILI CON QUESO

Looks so inviting. For even more zip use Pepper Jack cheese in place of Monterey Jack. Keep hot in chafing dish or fondue pot. A must for tortilla chips.

Skim evaporated milk	13¹/₂ oz.	385 mL
All-purpose flour	3 tbsp.	50 mL
Canned stewed tomatoes, drained, chopped and drained again	14 oz.	398 mL
Canned diced green chilies, drained	4 oz.	114 mL
Chili powder	1/2 tsp.	2 mL
Garlic powder	1/8 tsp.	0.5 mL
Cayenne pepper	1/4 tsp.	1 mL
Salt	1/2 tsp.	2 mL
Grated Monterey Jack cheese	3 cups	750 mL

(continued on next page)

Whisk evaporated milk into flour in large saucepan until no lumps remain. Heat and stir until boiling and thickened.

Add remaining 7 ingredients, stirring often until cheese is melted. Serve hot. Makes 4 cups (1 L).

1 tbsp. (15 mL): 28 Calories; 1.7 g Total Fat; 82 mg Sodium; 2 g Protein; 2 g Carbohydrate; trace Dietary Fiber

Pictured on page 35.

HOT BROCCOLI DIP

Chunky and cheesy. A different dip than the usual. Serve in chafing dish to keep hot. Have melba toast, crackers, corn chips, and toast rounds on the side.

Frozen chopped broccoli	**10 oz.**	**300 g**
Water	**1 cup**	**250 mL**
Hard margarine (or butter)	**½ cup**	**125 mL**
Chopped onion	**½ cup**	**125 mL**
Condensed cream of mushroom soup	**10 oz.**	**284 mL**
Grated medium Cheddar cheese	**2 cups**	**500 mL**
Garlic powder	**¼ tsp.**	**1 mL**
Canned mushroom pieces, drained and chopped	**10 oz.**	**284 mL**

Cook broccoli in water in small saucepan until barely tender. Drain. Chop larger pieces.

Melt margarine in large saucepan. Add onion. Sauté until soft and clear.

Add remaining 4 ingredients. Stir. Add broccoli mixture. Heat and stir until cheese is melted. Serve hot. Makes 4 cups (1 L).

2 tbsp. (30 mL): 69 Calories; 6 g Total Fat; 172 mg Sodium; 2 g Protein; 2 g Carbohydrate; trace Dietary Fiber

Paré Pointer

Business is when you don't have any of, you go out of.

GARBANZO DIP

Serve with crackers, or Tortilla Crisps, page 115.

Cooking oil	2 tbsp.	30 mL
Chopped onion	1 cup	250 mL
Small green pepper, chopped	1	1
Chopped celery	⅓ cup	75 mL
Canned garbanzo beans (chick peas), drained	14 oz.	398 mL
Lemon juice	4 tsp.	20 mL
Dried whole oregano	1 tsp.	5 mL
Garlic powder	¼ tsp.	1 mL
Salt	½ tsp.	2 mL
Pepper	⅛ tsp.	0.5 mL

Sliced ripe olives, for garnish

Heat cooking oil in non-stick frying pan. Add onion, green pepper and celery. Sauté for 10 to 15 minutes until soft.

Combine next 6 ingredients in food processor or blender. Add onion mixture. Process until smooth.

Just before serving, garnish with olive slices. Makes 1¾ cups (425 mL).

1 tbsp. (15 mL): *24 Calories; 1.2 g Total Fat; 65 mg Sodium; 1 g Protein; 3 g Carbohydrate; trace Dietary Fiber*

Pictured on page 35.

1. Chili Con Queso, page 32
2. Tortilla Crisps, page 115
3. Tortilla Chips, page 113
4. Kidney Bean Dip, page 37
5. Guacamole, page 32
6. Green Chili Bites, page 52
7. Garbanzo Dip, page 34
8. Cheesy Roll-Ups, page 97
9. Chili Rolls, page 101
10. Tortilla Roll-Ups, page 95

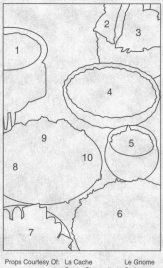

Props Courtesy Of: La Cache / Le Gnome / Scona Clayworks / Stokes / The Basket House / The Bay

If you're into "hot" you can add more cayenne pepper to this. It has a good flavor and an attractive browned top. Serve with tortilla chips, raw vegetables or corn chips.

BOTTOM LAYER

Canned kidney beans, drained	2 x 14 oz.	2 x 398 mL
Salsa (mild or medium)	6 tbsp.	100 mL
Sliced green onion	1/2 cup	125 mL
Chili powder	1 tsp.	5 mL
Onion powder	1/2 tsp.	2 mL
Garlic powder	1/4 tsp.	1 mL
White vinegar	1 tsp.	5 mL
Parsley flakes	2 tsp.	10 mL
Cayenne pepper	1/4 tsp.	1 mL
Salt	1/2 tsp.	2 mL

TOP LAYER

Grated medium Cheddar cheese	1 cup	250 mL
Grated Monterey Jack cheese	1 cup	250 mL
Chili powder	1 tsp.	5 mL

Bottom Layer: Mash kidney beans with fork in medium bowl.

Add next 9 ingredients. Mix well. Spread in ungreased 9 inch (22 cm) pie plate or shallow casserole.

Top Layer: Sprinkle with layer of Cheddar cheese, followed by layer of Monterey Jack cheese. Sprinkle with chili powder. Bake, uncovered, in 350°F (175°C) oven for about 30 minutes. Makes about 4 cups (1 L).

1 tbsp. (15 mL): 24 Calories; 1.2 g Total Fat; 79 mg Sodium; 2 g Protein; 2 g Carbohydrate; 1 g Dietary Fiber

Pictured on page 35.

Paré Pointer

When the little worm grows up he wants to join the apple core.

BLUE CHEESE DIP

A robust flavor yet not overbearing. Serve with chips or vegetables.
Great with Buffalo Wings, page 69.

Sour cream	1 cup	250 mL
Cream cheese, softened	4 oz.	125 g
Blue cheese, crumbled	1/2 cup	125 mL
Prepared horseradish	1 tsp.	5 mL
Lemon juice	1 tsp.	5 mL
Parsley flakes	1 tsp.	5 mL
Minced onion flakes	1 1/2 tsp.	7 mL
Salt	1/2 tsp.	2 mL

Mash all 8 ingredients in small bowl with fork or spoon. Beat with electric beater until fluffy. Makes $2\frac{1}{8}$ cups (530 mL).

1 tbsp. (15 mL): 30 Calories; 2.8 g Total Fat; 80 mg Sodium; 1 g Protein; 1 g Carbohydrate; trace Dietary Fiber

Pictured on page 107.

STRAWBERRY DIP

A pretty pink coating for fruit and cake.

Cut up fresh strawberries	1 cup	250 mL
Granulated sugar	1/4 cup	60 mL
Creamed cottage cheese, drained	1/3 cup	75 mL
Sour cream	1/3 cup	75 mL

Combine strawberries and sugar in small bowl. Stir. Let stand for 10 minutes, stirring twice. Drain in sieve. Place berries in blender.

Add cottage cheese and sour cream. Process until smooth. Turn into small bowl. Garnish as desired. Chill. Makes $1\frac{1}{2}$ cups (375 mL).

1 tbsp. (15 mL): 17 Calories; 0.5 g Total Fat; 15 mg Sodium; 1 g Protein; 3 g Carbohydrate; trace Dietary Fiber

Paré Pointer

When the prisoners put on a play, it was a cell out.

MANGO CHUTNEY DIP

This is also a good filling for Phyllo Nests, page 85. Fill each with 1½ tsp. (7 mL) filling. Serve with assorted crackers and chips.

Spreadable cream cheese	8 oz.	250 g
Mango chutney, chopped	⅓ cup	75 mL
Ground walnuts (or pecans)	½ cup	125 mL

Mix all 3 ingredients well in small bowl. Makes 1½ cups (375 mL).

1 tbsp. (15 mL): 51 Calories; 4.7 g Total Fat; 30 mg Sodium; 1 g Protein; 2 g Carbohydrate; trace Dietary Fiber

Pictured on front cover.

CRANBERRY DIP

So pretty for dunking fruit. But also a nice change with meat appetizers such as Party Meatballs, page 65, or Chicken Nuggets, page 62.

Canned cranberry jelly	14 oz.	398 mL
Lemon juice	2 tsp.	10 mL
Prepared mustard	½ tsp.	2 mL
Granulated sugar	2 tbsp.	30 mL

Mix all 4 ingredients in small bowl. Stir well. Makes 1½ cups (375 mL).

1 tbsp. (15 mL): 32 Calories; trace Total Fat; 7 mg Sodium; trace Protein; 8 g Carbohydrate; trace Dietary Fiber

Pictured on page 71.

FRUIT FROSTING

A dream dip that makes up quickly. Serve with fresh fruit.

Cream cheese, softened	8 oz.	250 g
Jar marshmallow cream	7 oz.	200 g
Milk	2 tbsp.	30 mL
Lemon juice	⅛ tsp.	0.5 mL

Beat all 4 ingredients together. Makes about 2 cups (500 mL).

1 tbsp. (15 mL): 45 Calories; 2.6 g Total Fat; 25 mg Sodium; 1 g Protein; 5 g Carbohydrate; 0 g Dietary Fiber

SPICY DIP

This cinnamon-flavored dip is just right for apples and other fruit. Place in a small dish in the center of a large plate or platter. Surround with cut fruit.

Sour cream	1 cup	250 mL
Brown sugar, packed	2 tbsp.	30 mL
Ground cinnamon	1/8 tsp.	0.5 mL
Brandy flavoring	1 tsp.	5 mL

Stir all 4 ingredients together in small bowl. Makes 1 cup (250 mL).

1 tbsp. (15 mL): 29 Calories; 2 g Total Fat; 7 mg Sodium; trace Protein; 2 g Carbohydrate; trace Dietary Fiber

MUSHROOM DIP

A chunky dip. Serve with potato chips or assorted crackers.

Hard margarine (or butter)	2 tbsp.	30 mL
Coarsely chopped fresh mushrooms (or sliced button mushrooms)	4 cups	1 L
Finely chopped onion	1/2 cup	125 mL
Worcestershire sauce	1 tbsp.	15 mL
Garlic powder	1/2 tsp.	2 mL
Light sour cream (see Note)	1 1/2 cups	375 mL
Dill weed	1 tsp.	5 mL

Melt margarine in large frying pan. Add mushrooms, onion, Worcestershire sauce and garlic powder. Sauté for 20 to 25 minutes, stirring often, until onion is soft and all liquid is evaporated.

Stir in sour cream and dill weed. Heat through. Turn into chafing dish. Makes 2 1/2 cups (625 mL).

2 tbsp. (30 mL): 32 Calories; 2.4 g Total Fat; 30 mg Sodium; 1 g Protein; 2 g Carbohydrate; trace Dietary Fiber

Note: Add up to 1/2 cup (125 mL) more sour cream if dip thickens while heating in chafing dish.

SIMPLE SWEET AND SOUR SAUCE

Perfect to dunk meatballs in this.

Brown sugar, packed	1 cup	250 mL
Cornstarch	2 tbsp.	30 mL
White vinegar	½ cup	125 mL
Pineapple juice (or water)	½ cup	125 mL

Stir brown sugar and cornstarch together in small saucepan.

Add vinegar and pineapple juice. Bring to a boil over medium stirring constantly until mixture is thickened. Makes 1⅓ cups (325 mL).

1 tbsp. (15 mL): 46 Calories; trace Total Fat; 3 mg Sodium; trace Protein; 12 g Carbohydrate; trace Dietary Fiber

Pictured on page 125.

MUSHROOM DILL DIP

Very tasty. Dill adds a nice touch. Serve with assorted crackers, chips or raw vegetables.

Hard margarine (or butter)	1 tsp.	5 mL
Finely chopped fresh mushrooms	1 cup	250 mL
Chopped green onion	½ cup	125 mL
Light cream cheese, softened	4 oz.	125 g
Light sour cream	⅓ cup	75 mL
Light salad dressing (or mayonnaise)	3 tbsp.	50 mL
Dill weed	1 tsp.	5 mL
Garlic powder	⅛ tsp.	0.5 mL
Salt	⅛ tsp.	0.5 mL

Heat margarine in frying pan. Add mushrooms and green onion. Sauté until golden. Cool.

Beat remaining 6 ingredients together well in medium bowl until creamy. Fold in mushroom mixture. Makes 1½ cups (375 mL).

1 tbsp. (15 mL): 15 Calories; 0.9 g Total Fat; 32 mg Sodium; 1 g Protein; 1 g Carbohydrate; trace Dietary Fiber

MEATBALL SAUCE

Double duty sauce. Drizzle over Party Meatballs, page 65, or other meatballs, or use as a dip.

Light sour cream	1 cup	250 mL
Prepared horseradish (not hot)	¼ cup	60 mL
Onion salt	¼ tsp.	1 mL
Seasoned salt	¼ tsp.	1 mL

Mix all 4 ingredients in small bowl. Cover. Refrigerate until ready to serve. Makes about 1¼ cups (300 mL).

1 tbsp. (15 mL): 12 Calories; 0.8 g Total Fat; 41 mg Sodium; trace Protein; 1 g Carbohydrate; trace Dietary Fiber

Pictured on page 71.

ORANGE COCONUT FRUIT DIP

Pale yellow in color. Serve with fruit pieces.

Creamed cottage cheese	2 cups	500 mL
Sour cream	¼ cup	60 mL
Frozen concentrated orange juice	2 tbsp.	30 mL
Granulated sugar	2 tbsp.	30 mL
Fine (or medium) coconut	¼ cup	60 mL
Finely grated orange peel, for garnish		

Measure first 4 ingredients into blender. Process until smooth. Turn into medium bowl.

Stir in coconut. Garnish with orange peel. Makes 1½ cups (375 mL).

1 tbsp. (15 mL): 30 Calories; 1.2 g Total Fat; 81 mg Sodium; 3 g Protein; 2 g Carbohydrate; trace Dietary Fiber

Paré Pointer

When the tailor couldn't find his scissors his pet frog said, "Rippit, rippit."

DOUBLE DILL DIP

Double the pleasure. A treat with fresh veggies.

Cream cheese, softened	4 oz.	125 g
Sour cream	2 cups	500 mL
Lemon juice	1 tsp.	5 mL
Parsley flakes	2 tsp.	10 mL
Onion flakes	2 tsp.	10 mL
Dill weed	2 tsp.	10 mL
Onion salt	1 tsp.	5 mL
Garlic powder	½ tsp.	2 mL
Jar of tangy dill bits, drained	13½ oz.	375 mL

Combine first 8 ingredients in blender. Process until smooth. Turn into medium bowl.

Stir in dill bits. Makes 4½ cups (1.1 L).

1 tbsp. (15 mL): 17 Calories; 1.5 g Total Fat; 68 mg Sodium; trace Protein; 1 g Carbohydrate; trace Dietary Fiber

ARTICHOKE DIP

Exceptionally good. Serve with chips or bread chunks.

Canned artichoke hearts, drained and finely chopped	14 oz.	398 mL
Salad dressing (or mayonnaise)	¾ cup	175 mL
Sour cream	¼ cup	60 mL
Grated Parmesan cheese	½ cup	125 mL
Onion salt	1/16 tsp.	0.5 mL
Garlic powder	1/16 tsp.	0.5 mL
Hot pepper sauce	1/16 tsp.	0.5 mL
Sliced (or slivered) almonds, toasted in 350°F (175°C) oven for about 5 minutes	½ cup	125 mL
Paprika	½ tsp.	2 mL

Mix first 7 ingredients well in medium bowl. Turn into ungreased 9 inch (22 cm) pie plate. Bake, uncovered, in 350°F (175°C) oven for 15 to 20 minutes until hot.

Sprinkle dip with almonds and paprika. Makes 2 cups (500 mL).

1 tbsp. (15 mL): 48 Calories; 4.1 g Total Fat; 87 mg Sodium; 1 g Protein; 2 g Carbohydrate; 1 g Dietary Fiber

HERB DIP

Vegetables and chips go well with this dip.

Cream cheese, softened	8 oz.	250 g
Plain yogurt	1 cup	250 mL
Salad dressing (or mayonnaise)	1/4 cup	60 mL
Dried chopped chives	1 tbsp.	15 mL
Parsley flakes	1 tsp.	5 mL
Celery salt	1/2 tsp.	2 mL
Salt	1/4 tsp.	1 mL
Dried thyme	1/4 tsp.	1 mL
Garlic powder	1/4 tsp.	1 mL
Dried sweet basil	1/4 tsp.	1 mL
Onion powder	1/4 tsp.	1 mL

Paprika, for garnish

Beat first 11 ingredients together in small bowl until smooth. Chill for at least 2 hours before serving.

Garnish with paprika. Makes generous 2 cups (500 mL).

1 tbsp. (15 mL): 41 Calories; 3.7 g Total Fat; 80 mg Sodium; 1 g Protein; 1 g Carbohydrate; trace Dietary Fiber

SWEET CURRY DIP

Serve with assorted crackers, chips, raw vegetables or fresh fruit. Curry flavor is middle of the road.

Low-fat sweetened condensed milk	11 oz.	300 mL
White vinegar	1/3 cup	75 mL
Dry mustard	3/4 tsp.	4 mL
Curry powder, more or less	3/4 tsp.	4 mL
Garlic powder	1/8 tsp.	0.5 mL

Stir all 5 ingredients together well in small bowl. Makes 1 1/3 cups (325 mL).

1 tbsp. (15 mL): 60 Calories; 0.7 g Total Fat; 23 mg Sodium; 1 g Protein; 10 g Carbohydrate; trace Dietary Fiber

Pictured on page 53.

A merry-go-round of red-edged apple slices makes for a very showy appetizer. Invite guests to help themselves. This is good enough to be dessert.

Light cream cheese, softened	8 oz.	250 g
Brown sugar, packed	¾ cup	175 mL
Vanilla	1 tbsp.	15 mL
Red-skinned apples, cut into thin wedges (about 32 in total)	2	2
Lemon juice	¼ cup	60 mL

Beat cream cheese, brown sugar and vanilla in medium bowl until smooth. Turn into small serving dish on plate.

Dip apple wedges into lemon juice to prevent browning. Arrange on plate, surrounding dip. Makes 1 cup (250 mL).

1 tbsp. (15 mL) plus 2 apple wedges: 67 Calories; 1.3 g Total Fat; 75 mg Sodium; 1 g Protein; 13 g Carbohydrate; trace Dietary Fiber

The color of daffodils with orange and green flecks. Exceptionally good. Serve with assorted raw vegetables, cut bite size.

Chopped onion	1 tbsp.	15 mL
Grated carrot, packed	⅓ cup	75 mL
Medium green pepper, cut up	½	½
White vinegar	1 tbsp.	15 mL
Salad dressing (or mayonnaise)	½ cup	125 mL
Process yellow cheese spread	½ cup	125 mL

Place first 4 ingredients in blender. Process until crumbly smooth, not puréed.

Add salad dressing and cheese. Stir well. Best served same day. Makes generous 1⅓ cups (325 mL).

1 tbsp. (15 mL): 47 Calories; 4 g Total Fat; 133 mg Sodium; 1 g Protein; 2 g Carbohydrate; trace Dietary Fiber

HOT CRAB DIP

Just the right amount of zip to this good dip. Serve hot with assorted crackers.

Cream cheese, softened	8 oz.	250 g
White (or alcohol-free white) wine	1 tbsp.	15 mL
Salad dressing (or mayonnaise)	2 tbsp.	30 mL
Prepared mustard	½ tsp.	2 mL
Onion flakes	2 tsp.	10 mL
Seasoned salt	½ tsp.	2 mL
Canned crabmeat, drained and cartilage removed	5 oz.	142 g

Place first 6 ingredients in small bowl. Beat until smooth. Turn into double boiler.

Fold crabmeat into cream cheese mixture using a spatula. Heat over simmering water. Makes 1⅔ cups (400 mL).

1 tbsp. (15 mL): 41 Calories; 3.7 g Total Fat; 93 mg Sodium; 1 g Protein; 1 g Carbohydrate; trace Dietary Fiber

BACON DIP

Smoky, creamy taste. Quite thick. Creamy white with green and brown bits. Serve with fresh assorted vegetables and potato chips. Also good spread on crackers.

Bacon slices, diced, cooked and drained (½ lb., 225 g)	8	8
Sour cream	⅔ cup	150 mL
Parsley flakes	1 tsp.	5 mL
Onion powder	⅛ tsp.	0.5 mL
Garlic salt	⅛ tsp.	0.5 mL
Cayenne pepper	1/16 tsp.	0.5 mL

Stir all 6 ingredients together in small bowl. Cover. Store in refrigerator overnight to blend flavors. Makes 1 cup (250 mL).

1 tbsp. (15 mL): 33 Calories; 2.9 g Total Fat; 63 mg Sodium; 1 g Protein; trace Carbohydrate; trace Dietary Fiber

GOUDA EN CROÛTE

An elegant first course, especially the mini cheeses.

PASTRY

All-purpose flour	¾ cup	175 mL
Brown sugar, packed	1 tsp.	5 mL
Baking powder	¼ tsp.	1 mL
Salt	¼ tsp.	1 mL
Hard margarine (or butter)	6 tbsp.	100 mL
Cold water	2 tbsp.	30 mL
Gouda cheese rounds, red wax removed	2 x 7 oz.	2 x 200 g
Ground walnuts (or pecans)	½ cup	125 mL

Pastry: Stir flour, brown sugar, baking powder and salt in medium bowl. Cut in margarine with pastry blender until mixture is crumbly.

Add cold water. Mix dough into a ball, adding a bit more water if needed. Divide into 4 equal portions. Roll out each portion on lightly floured surface into 6 inch (15 cm) circles.

Set cheese rounds on 2 pastry circles. Cover tops of cheese with walnuts. Set remaining 2 pastry circles in place over walnuts. Moisten edges with water. Crimp together to seal. Bake in 425°F (220°C) oven for 20 to 25 minutes until lightly browned. Each round cuts into 10 wedges, for a total of 20.

1 wedge: 139 Calories; 10.7 g Total Fat; 243 mg Sodium; 6 g Protein; 5 g Carbohydrate; trace Dietary Fiber

BABY GOUDAS EN CROÛTE:
Pastry, see above

Baby Gouda cheese rounds, red wax removed	6 x ¾ oz.	6 x 21 g
Ground walnuts (or pecans)	2 tbsp.	30 mL

Divide pastry into 12 portions. Roll out each portion on lightly floured surface into 3 inch (7.5 cm) circles.

Place 1 baby Gouda on each of 6 pastry circles. Sprinkle with 1 tsp. (5 mL) walnuts. Cover with remaining 6 pastry circles. Moisten edges with water. Crimp together to seal. Bake in 425°F (220°C) oven for 12 to 15 minutes. Makes 6.

BRIE EN CROÛTE: Omit Gouda cheese and use Brie instead.

CRAB-STUFFED EGGS

Always a winner on an appetizer tray. Also used as an extra for a cold salad plate. Cut eggs lengthwise, or crosswise—either way works just fine.

Large hard-boiled eggs, peeled	12	12
Mayonnaise (not salad dressing)	1/3 cup	75 mL
Prepared mustard	1/2 tsp.	2 mL
Lemon juice	1/2 tsp.	2 mL
Dill weed	1/8 tsp.	0.5 mL
Seasoned salt	1/4 tsp.	1 mL
Chopped chives	2 tsp.	10 mL
Dried whole oregano	1/8 tsp.	0.5 mL
Canned crabmeat, drained and cartilage removed	1 cup	250 mL
Paprika, sprinkle		

Cut eggs in half crosswise. Carefully remove yolks to small bowl. Place egg white halves on flat surface. Set aside. Mash yolks with fork.

Add next 8 ingredients. Mix well. If too dry, add a bit of milk. Makes 2 cups (500 mL) filling. Fill egg white halves. A pastry tube makes an attractive design.

Sprinkle with paprika. Makes 24.

1 stuffed egg half: 67 Calories; 5.3 g Total Fat; 106 mg Sodium; 4 g Protein; trace Carbohydrate; trace Dietary Fiber

Pictured on page 53.

SHRIMP-STUFFED EGGS: Use chopped cooked fresh (or frozen, thawed) shrimp instead of crabmeat.

FROZEN CHEESE PUFFS

Rich-tasting pastry encloses green olives. These look great.

Hard margarine (or butter), softened	1/2 cup	125 mL
All-purpose flour	1 cup	250 mL
Grated sharp Cheddar cheese, room temperature	2 cups	500 mL
Small pimiento-stuffed green olives	30	30

(continued on next page)

Work margarine and flour together well in large bowl.

Add cheese. Mix well, warming with your hands to work mixture together. Divide and roll into 1 inch (2.5 cm) balls.

Flatten each ball and shape around olive, sealing dough together. Freeze in single layer on baking sheet. Store in plastic bag or container in freezer. Bake from frozen state on ungreased baking sheet in 375°F (190°C) oven for 10 to 15 minutes until puffy and lightly browned. Makes 2½ dozen.

1 cheese puff: 117 Calories; 10.3 g Total Fat; 904 mg Sodium; 3 g Protein; 4 g Carbohydrate; 2 g Dietary Fiber

CHEESE THINS

Large thin wafers that are crispy good. Makes a showy basketful. Serve with Double Dill Dip, page 43.

All-purpose flour	2 cups	500 mL
Grated sharp Cheddar cheese	1 cup	250 mL
Granulated sugar	1 tbsp.	15 mL
Baking soda	½ tsp.	2 mL
Salt	½ tsp.	2 mL
Onion powder	¼ tsp.	1 mL
Cayenne pepper	1/16 tsp.	0.5 mL
Cooking oil	¼ cup	60 mL
Water	½ cup	125 mL

Measure first 7 ingredients into medium bowl. Stir well.

Add cooking oil and water. Mix until dough forms a ball. Cover. Let stand for 20 minutes. Divide into 4 portions. Roll out 1 portion paper thin on lightly floured surface. Cut into 8 wedges. Arrange wedges on ungreased baking sheet. Bake in 375°F (190°C) oven for about 10 minutes until crisp and browned. Repeat for remaining dough. Makes 32 wedges.

1 wedge: 63 Calories; 3.1 g Total Fat; 87 mg Sodium; 2 g Protein; 7 g Carbohydrate; trace Dietary Fiber

Paré Pointer

Woman complaining to marriage counselor about her husband: "When he won a trip for two to Hawaii, he went twice!"

MINI CHEESE BALLS

Offer a variety of tastes and colors with these tiny individual balls.

Grated sharp Cheddar cheese	2 cups	500 mL
Cream cheese, softened	4 oz.	125 g
Worcestershire sauce	½ tsp.	2 mL
Lemon juice	1 tsp.	5 mL
Seasoned salt	½ tsp.	2 mL
COATINGS		
Toasted sesame seeds	2 tbsp.	30 mL
Chili powder	2 tsp.	10 mL
Dill weed	2 tsp.	10 mL

Combine first 5 ingredients in medium bowl. Mix. Shape into 24 walnut-size balls.

Coatings: Roll ⅓ of balls in sesame seeds. Roll ⅓ of balls in chili powder until dark. Roll remaining ⅓ of balls in dill weed. If you prefer, all balls can be rolled to look the same. Makes 24.

1 cheese ball: 64 Calories; 5.5 g Total Fat; 110 mg Sodium; 3 g Protein; 1 g Carbohydrate; trace Dietary Fiber

Pictured on page 53.

SPINACH SQUARES

Cheese and spinach are a natural combination.

Hard margarine (or butter)	¼ cup	60 mL
Large eggs	3	3
All-purpose flour	1 cup	250 mL
Milk	1 cup	250 mL
Salt	1 tsp.	5 mL
Baking powder	1 tsp.	5 mL
Grated Havarti cheese	4 cups	1 L
Frozen chopped spinach, thawed and squeezed dry	2 × 10 oz.	2 × 300 g

Melt margarine in large saucepan.

Add next 5 ingredients. Mix.

(continued on next page)

Add cheese and spinach. Stir together. Turn into greased 9 x 13 inch (22 x 33 cm) pan. Bake in 350°F (175°C) oven for about 35 minutes until set and browned. Cool. Cuts into 54 squares.

1 square: 56 Calories; 3.6 g Total Fat; 142 mg Sodium; 3 g Protein; 3 g Carbohydrate; trace Dietary Fiber

CRISPY CHEESE WAFERS

These deliver crunch and heat. A winner.

Hard margarine (or butter), softened	**1 cup**	**250 mL**
Grated medium Cheddar cheese, room temperature	**2 cups**	**500 mL**
Cayenne pepper	**½ tsp.**	**2 mL**
Salt	**½ tsp.**	**2 mL**
All-purpose flour	**2 cups**	**500 mL**
Crisp rice cereal	**2 cups**	**500 mL**

Cream margarine and cheese in large bowl. Mix in cayenne pepper and salt.

Add flour. Work in until dough is soft.

Add cereal. Mix. Shape into 2 rolls about 2 inches (5 cm) in diameter. Roll up in waxed paper. Chill for 2 hours. Slice ¼ inch (6 mm) thick.

Arrange on well-greased baking sheet. Bake in 350°F (175°C) oven for 15 to 16 minutes until browned. Makes about 60.

1 wafer: 65 Calories; 4.6 g Total Fat; 96 mg Sodium; 2 g Protein; 4 g Carbohydrate; trace Dietary Fiber

Paré Pointer

Yeast is one of the major causes of inflation.

GREEN CHILI BITES

This really is yummy. Both spicy-hot and oven-hot.

Large eggs	5	5
All-purpose flour	¼ cup	60 mL
Baking powder	½ tsp.	2 mL
Salt	¼ tsp.	1 mL
Pepper	⅛ tsp.	0.5 mL
Hard margarine (or butter), melted	¼ cup	60 mL
Canned diced green chilies, drained	4 oz.	114 mL
Grated Monterey Jack cheese	2 cups	500 mL
Creamed cottage cheese, mashed with fork	1 cup	250 mL
Hot pepper sauce	¼ tsp.	1 mL

Beat eggs in medium bowl until frothy. Add flour, baking powder, salt, pepper, and margarine. Beat well.

Stir in green chilies, Monterey Jack cheese, cottage cheese and hot pepper sauce. Pour into greased 9 x 9 inch (22 x 22 cm) square pan. Bake in 350°F (175°C) oven for 35 to 45 minutes until lightly browned and set. Serve hot. Cuts into 36 appetizer squares, or serves 9 as a main course starter.

1 appetizer square: *56 Calories; 4.2 g Total Fat; 126 mg Sodium; 3 g Protein; 1 g Carbohydrate; trace Dietary Fiber*

Pictured on page 35.

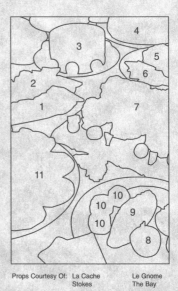

1. Ham Turnovers, page 91
2. Cheese Triangles, page 93
3. Sweet Curry Dip, page 44
4. Gougère, page 55
5. Apricot Cheese Spread, page 122
6. Party Crackers, page 117
7. Salad Horns, page 138
8. Crab-Stuffed Eggs, page 48
9. Bruschetta Brie, page 124
10. Mini Cheese Balls, page 50
11. Dolmades, page 104

Props Courtesy Of: La Cache   Le Gnome
Stokes   The Bay

GOUGÈRE

This is a sort of cheese cake from the Burgundy region in France. Goo-ZHAIR resembles cream puffs or Yorkshire Pudding. Can be served hot or cold, but should be cut first as it is a bit greasy in the hands because of the cheese.

Water	**1 cup**	**250 mL**
Hard margarine (or butter)	**½ cup**	**125 mL**
Salt	**1 tsp.**	**5 mL**
All-purpose flour	**1 cup**	**250 mL**
Large eggs	**4**	**4**
Grated Gruyère cheese	**1 cup**	**250 mL**
Large egg, fork-beaten, for topping	**1**	**1**
Grated Gruyère cheese, for topping	**¼ cup**	**60 mL**

Bring water, margarine and salt to a boil in medium saucepan.

Add flour all at once. Stir briskly until mixture is smooth and thickened and pulls away from sides of pan. Remove from heat.

Add eggs, 1 at a time, beating thoroughly with a spoon after each addition.

Add first amount of cheese. Work into mixture. Using greased 9 or 10 inch (22 or 25 cm) pie plate, pipe or pile dough into puffs around edge. Fill in center and pile on top as necessary. Brush top with egg.

Sprinkle with second amount of Gruyère cheese. Bake in 400°F (205°C) oven for 30 to 35 minutes until puffed and browned. Serve hot or cold. Cuts into 16 wedges.

1 wedge: 145 Calories; 10.6 g Total Fat; 291 mg Sodium; 6 g Protein; 7 g Carbohydrate; trace Dietary Fiber

Pictured on page 53.

Paré Pointer

You better keep going even if you are on the right track. You could get run over.

MARINATED SHRIMP

Takes extra time to get this into the refrigerator but it's ready to serve with barely any effort. Serve with wooden picks.

Water	2½ qts.	2.5 L
Salt	4 tsp.	20 mL
Mustard seed	1 tsp.	5 mL
Bay leaves	3	3
Whole allspice	1 tsp.	5 mL
Whole cloves	1 tsp.	5 mL
Dried crushed chilies	2 tsp.	10 mL
Whole peppercorns	1 tsp.	5 mL
Fresh medium shrimp in shells (70-80 shrimp)	2 lbs.	900 g
MARINADE		
Cooking oil	¼ cup	60 mL
White vinegar	⅓ cup	75 mL
Water	½ cup	125 mL
Celery seed	1 tsp.	5 mL
Celery salt	½ tsp.	2 mL
Cayenne pepper	⅛ tsp.	0.5 mL
Salt	½ tsp.	2 mL
Worcestershire sauce	2 tbsp.	30 mL
Prepared mustard	1 tsp.	5 mL
Large onion, thinly sliced	1	1

Heat water and salt in large pot or Dutch oven until boiling.

Tie next 6 ingredients in double layer of cheesecloth. Add to boiling water.

Add shrimp. Return to a boil. Boil, uncovered, for 2 to 3 minutes until shrimp are curled and pinkish. Drain. Cool and shell. Discard cheesecloth bag and contents.

Marinade: Mix first 9 ingredients in small bowl. Layer ½ of shrimp in large bowl.

Add ½ of onion over top. Cover with second ½ of shrimp and remaining ½ of onion. Pour marinade over all. Cover. Let stand in refrigerator for at least 24 hours. Turn out into dish or onto large platter. Makes about 75.

1 shrimp (with marinade): 20 Calories; 0.9 g Total Fat; 56 mg Sodium; 3 g Protein; trace Carbohydrate; trace Dietary Fiber

Pictured on page 89.

This makes a large quantity. Filling freezes well, allowing you to prepare as much as you like.

Boiling water	1 tbsp.	15 mL
Seafood bouillon powder	1 tsp.	5 mL
Cream cheese, softened	8 oz.	250 g
Pepper	$\frac{1}{16}$ tsp.	0.5 mL
Worcestershire sauce	$\frac{1}{8}$ tsp.	0.5 mL
Onion powder	$\frac{1}{4}$ tsp.	1 mL
Parsley flakes	1 tsp.	5 mL
Prepared horseradish	$\frac{1}{2}$ tsp.	2 mL
Balsamic vinegar (or lemon juice)	1 tsp.	5 mL
Cooked fresh (or frozen cooked, thawed) shrimp, chopped	6 oz.	170 g
Cherry tomatoes	36	36

Stir boiling water into bouillon powder in small bowl. Add next 7 ingredients. Mash together well with fork.

Add shrimp. Mix well. Makes 1½ cups (375 mL) filling.

Cut tomatoes in half crosswise. Scoop out seeds. Stuff with cream cheese filling by piping or spooning 1 tsp. (5 mL) into each half. Makes 72.

1 stuffed tomato half: 16 Calories; 1.3 g Total Fat; 25 mg Sodium; 1 g Protein; trace Carbohydrate; trace Dietary Fiber

Pictured on front cover.

Paré Pointer

You can eat beef all your life and be as strong as an ox, but you can eat fish all your life and not swim a stroke.

SHRIMP KABOBS

Succulent. Fancy to look at, but easy to make ahead of time.

Cooking oil	1 tbsp.	15 mL
Hard margarine (or butter), melted	3 tbsp.	50 mL
Lemon juice	1 tbsp.	15 mL
Soy sauce	1 tbsp.	15 mL
Parsley flakes	1 tbsp.	15 mL
Garlic salt	1/8 tsp.	0.5 mL
Fresh medium shrimp, peeled and deveined	24	24

Combine first 6 ingredients in medium bowl. Stir.

Add shrimp. Place in plastic bag. Close tightly. Marinate in refrigerator for 20 minutes, turning bag often. Empty contents into medium-hot frying pan. Stir-fry for about 5 minutes until shrimp are curled and pinkish. Cool shrimp and marinade. Soak twelve 4 inch (10 cm) wooden skewers in water for 10 minutes. Place 2 shrimp on each skewer. Chill skewers and marinade until just before serving. When ready to serve, heat marinade. Place skewers on ungreased baking sheet. Brush shrimp with marinade. Discard any remaining marinade. Heat kabobs in 400°F (205°C) oven for 3 to 5 minutes until hot. Makes 12.

1 kabob: 43 Calories; 3.9 g Total Fat; 148 mg Sodium; 2 g Protein; trace Carbohydrate; trace Dietary Fiber

Pictured on page 71.

CRAB RANGOON

Serve these wontons hot from the fresh or frozen state. Try dipping in Simple Sweet And Sour Sauce, page 41.

Cream cheese, softened	4 oz.	125 g
Garlic cloves, minced (or 1/4-1/2 tsp., 1-2 mL, garlic powder)	1-2	1-2
Salt	1/4 tsp.	1 mL
Hot pepper sauce	1/8 tsp.	0.5 mL
Green onions, thinly sliced	2	2
Canned crabmeat, drained and cartilage removed	1 cup	250 mL
Square wonton wrappers	48	48
Cooking oil, for deep-frying		

(continued on next page)

Mash cream cheese, garlic, salt and hot pepper sauce well in small bowl. Mix in green onion and crabmeat.

❶ Place about 1 tsp. (5 mL) filling in center of each wrapper. Moisten 2 adjoining edges. ❷ Fold center moistened point over filling, tucking point under filling. ❸ Bring remaining 2 moistened corners to center just above tucked edge, overlapping slightly. Press down on points to seal.

Deep-fry a few at a time in hot 375°F (190°C) cooking oil for about 1 minute until golden brown. Serve immediately, or cool and freeze at this point. Reheat on greased baking sheet in 400°F (205°C) oven for about 5 minutes until hot. Makes 48.

1 appetizer: *23 Calories; 1.6 g Total Fat; 54 mg Sodium; 1 g Protein; 1 g Carbohydrate; trace Dietary Fiber*

Pictured on page 125.

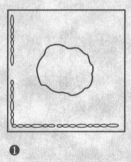
❶

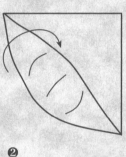
❷

❸

TRIPLE SATAY

Wonderful flavor. Melt-in-your-mouth tender.

Boneless, skinless chicken breast halves (about 2), cut into ¾ inch (2 cm) cubes	½ lb.	225 g
Beef tenderloin, cut into ¾ inch (2 cm) cubes	½ lb.	225 g
Pork tenderloin, cut into ¾ inch (2 cm) cubes	½ lb.	225 g
Soy sauce	½ cup	125 mL
Cooking oil	2 tbsp.	30 mL
White vinegar	¼ cup	60 mL
Granulated sugar	¼ cup	60 mL
Ground ginger	½ tsp.	2 mL
Garlic powder	¼ tsp.	1 mL
Chili powder	½ tsp.	2 mL
SATAY SAUCE		
Smooth peanut butter	½ cup	125 mL
Soy sauce	1 tbsp.	15 mL
Chili sauce	2 tbsp.	30 mL
Dried crushed chilies	¼ tsp.	1 mL
Fine coconut	1 tbsp.	15 mL
Brown sugar, packed	2 tbsp.	30 mL
Onion powder	¼ tsp.	1 mL
Skim evaporated milk	½ cup	125 mL

Put chicken, beef and pork cubes into medium bowl with tight fitting lid, or into 3 separate bowls if desired.

Mix remaining 7 ingredients in small bowl. Pour over cubes. Cover. Shake or turn to coat. Chill for several hours or overnight. Soak eighteen 4 inch (10 cm) wooden skewers in water for 10 minutes. Thread 1 cube of each meat onto each skewer. Lay on ungreased broiler tray. Broil about 4 inches (10 cm) from heat for about 5 minutes, turning at half-time, until cooked.

Satay Sauce: Mix all 8 ingredients in medium saucepan. Heat and stir until boiling. Simmer for 5 minutes, stirring constantly. Makes 1 cup (250 mL) sauce. Serve in small bowl with kabobs. Makes 18.

1 kabob (with sauce): 134 Calories; 6.7 g Total Fat; 608 mg Sodium; 11 g Protein; 8 g Carbohydrate; 1 g Dietary Fiber

Pictured on page 71.

SNAP WINGS

And a snap to make. Good taste. Sweet and dark soy flavor.

Whole chicken wings (or drumettes)	3 lbs.	1.4 kg
Apple juice	½ cup	125 mL
Soy sauce	½ cup	125 mL
Brown sugar, packed	½ cup	125 mL
Garlic powder (optional)	⅛ tsp.	0.5 mL

Remove wing tips and discard. Cut wings apart at joint. Arrange in single layer on greased baking sheet with sides or pan lined with greased foil.

Stir remaining 4 ingredients together well in medium bowl. Pour over chicken. Bake, uncovered, in 400°F (205°C) oven for about 1 hour, basting frequently, until sticky and glazed. Makes about 36 wing pieces or 24 drumettes.

1 piece (with sauce): 100 Calories; 6.1 g Total Fat; 270 mg Sodium; 7 g Protein; 4 g Carbohydrate; trace Dietary Fiber

Pictured on page 71.

LITTLE SMOKIES

Caramel-colored sauce sticks well to each sausage. Very quick and easy.

Brown sugar, packed	½ cup	125 mL
All-purpose flour	2 tbsp.	30 mL
White vinegar	⅓ cup	75 mL
Pineapple juice	½ cup	125 mL
Soy sauce	2 tsp.	10 mL
Ketchup	1 tsp.	5 mL
Smoked cocktail sausages	1½ lbs.	680 g

Stir brown sugar and flour in small saucepan until well mixed.

Add vinegar, pineapple juice, soy sauce, and ketchup. Heat and stir until sauce is boiling and thickened.

Add sausages. Cover. Simmer to heat through. Serve in chafing dish. Makes about 48.

1 sausage (with sauce): 52 Calories; 3.6 g Total Fat; 152 mg Sodium; 2 g Protein; 3 g Carbohydrate; trace Dietary Fiber

Pictured on page 89.

CHICKEN NUGGETS

Ground turkey may also be used for this. Bite-size balls are very tasty.

Ground raw chicken	1 lb.	454 g
Onion flakes	2 tsp.	10 mL
Large egg	1	1
Fine dry bread crumbs	½ cup	125 mL
Milk	⅓ cup	75 mL
Dried thyme	½ tsp.	2 mL
Salt	¾ tsp.	4 mL
Salad dressing (or mayonnaise)	¼ cup	60 mL
Milk	2 tbsp.	30 mL
Fine dry bread crumbs	⅔ cup	150 mL
Paprika	1 tsp.	5 mL

Combine first 7 ingredients in medium bowl. Mix well. Let chill in refrigerator for about 1 hour to firm for easier rolling. Shape into 1 inch (2.5 cm) balls.

Mix salad dressing and second amount of milk in small bowl.

Stir second amount of bread crumbs and paprika together. Dip chicken balls into salad dressing mixture then coat with crumb mixture. Arrange in single layer on greased baking sheet or pan lined with greased foil. Bake in 425°F (220°C) oven for 15 to 20 minutes until cooked. Makes about 36.

1 nugget: 41 Calories; 1.4 g Total Fat; 106 mg Sodium; 4 g Protein; 3 g Carbohydrate; trace Dietary Fiber

Pictured on page 71.

CRUSTY PARMESAN WINGS

Flavorful Parmesan gives wings a real lift. Great for munching.

Grated Parmesan cheese	1 cup	250 mL
Fine dry bread crumbs	½ cup	125 mL
Paprika	1½ tsp.	7 mL
Golden Italian dressing	¾ cup	175 mL
Whole chicken wings (or drumettes)	3 lbs.	1.4 kg

(continued on next page)

Combine cheese, bread crumbs and paprika in small bowl. Stir well.

Pour dressing into separate small bowl.

Remove wing tips and discard. Cut wings apart at joint. Dip each piece into dressing then coat with cheese mixture. Arrange in single layer on greased baking sheet with sides or pan lined with greased foil. Bake in 350°F (175°C) oven for about 45 minutes until tender. Serve warm. These may be prepared ahead. Reheat in 350°F (175°C) oven for about 10 minutes until hot. Makes about 36 wing pieces or 24 drumettes.

1 coated piece: 136 Calories; 10.6 g Total Fat; 176 mg Sodium; 8 g Protein; 2 g Carbohydrate; trace Dietary Fiber

Pictured on page 71.

CHICKEN WINGS SESAME

The sesame flavor comes through well in these delicious morsels. Nice in appearance too.

Large eggs	2	2
Prepared mustard	2 tbsp.	30 mL
Cooking oil	2 tbsp.	30 mL
Brown sugar, packed	2 tbsp.	30 mL
Salt	1 tsp.	5 mL
Fine dry bread crumbs	1¼ cups	300 mL
Sesame seeds	⅓ cup	75 mL
Whole chicken wings (or drumettes)	3 lbs.	1.4 kg

Beat eggs with whisk or fork in small bowl. Add next 4 ingredients. Mix well.

Mix bread crumbs and sesame seeds in separate small bowl.

Remove wing tips and discard. Cut wings apart at joint. Dip pieces into egg mixture then into bread crumb mixture. Arrange in single layer on greased baking sheet with sides or pan lined with greased foil. Bake in 425°F (220°C) oven for 25 to 30 minutes, turning at half-time. Makes about 36 wing pieces or 24 drumettes.

1 coated piece: 123 Calories; 8.1 g Total Fat; 148 mg Sodium; 8 g Protein; 4 g Carbohydrate; trace Dietary Fiber

Pictured on page 71.

SWEET AND SOUR SAUSAGE BALLS

Sauce is more sweet than sour.

Sausage meat	2 lbs.	900 g
Fine dry bread crumbs	²/₃ cup	150 mL
Large egg, fork-beaten	1	1
SWEET AND SOUR SAUCE		
Canned pineapple tidbits, drained	14 oz.	398 mL
Ketchup	³/₄ cup	175 mL
Chili sauce	¹/₂ cup	125 mL
Brown sugar, packed	¹/₃ cup	75 mL
Soy sauce	1 tbsp.	15 mL
Lemon juice	1 tbsp.	15 mL
Garlic powder	¹/₈ tsp.	0.5 mL
Ground ginger	¹/₈ tsp.	0.5 mL

Shape sausage meat into 1 inch (2.5 cm) balls. Arrange in single layer on ungreased baking sheet. Bake in 350°F (175°C) oven for 15 to 20 minutes. Drain well.

Sweet And Sour Sauce: Combine all 8 ingredients in large frying pan. Add cooked sausage balls. Bring sauce to a boil. When hot, turn into chafing dish. Makes about 40.

1 ball (with sauce): 72 Calories; 4.1 g Total Fat; 240 mg Sodium; 2 g Protein; 7 g Carbohydrate; trace Dietary Fiber

Pictured on page 107.

SZECHUAN SATAY

So rich looking. Delicious ginger and garlic flavors.

Beef sirloin steak	1 lb.	454 g
Soy sauce	3 tbsp.	50 mL
Granulated sugar	2 tsp.	10 mL
Minced gingerroot	1 tbsp.	15 mL
Garlic powder (or 2 cloves, minced)	¹/₂ tsp.	2 mL
Dried crushed chilies	¹/₂ tsp.	2 mL

Cut steak into ¹/₈ inch (3 mm) thick slices. Cut long slices in half. This is easier to do if steak is partially frozen.

Stir remaining 5 ingredients in medium bowl. Add meat strips. Stir to coat. Let stand for 30 minutes, stirring often.

(continued on next page)

Soak twenty-six 4 inch (10 cm) wooden skewers in water for 10 minutes. Thread skewers with meat strips. Place on wire rack over baking sheet with sides. Broil about 5 inches (12.5 cm) from heat for 6 to 8 minutes, turning once, until medium doneness. When ready to serve, set on greased baking sheet. Bake in 400°F (205°C) oven for 5 minutes until hot. Makes about 26.

1 kabob: 24 Calories; 0.7 g Total Fat; 129 mg Sodium; 4 g Protein; 1 g Carbohydrate; trace Dietary Fiber

Pictured on page 71.

PARTY MEATBALLS

Contains beef and turkey. Gently spiced. Serve with cocktail picks.

Fine dry bread crumbs	**²⁄₃ cup**	**150 mL**
Salt	**1¹⁄₂ tsp.**	**7 mL**
Pepper	**¹⁄₄ tsp.**	**1 mL**
Garlic powder	**¹⁄₂ tsp.**	**2 mL**
Onion powder	**¹⁄₂ tsp.**	**2 mL**
Ground nutmeg, large measure	**¹⁄₄ tsp.**	**1 mL**
Large egg, fork-beaten	**1**	**1**
Water	**¹⁄₄ cup**	**60 mL**
Lean ground beef	**1 lb.**	**454 g**
Lean ground raw turkey	**1 lb.**	**454 g**

Combine first 6 ingredients in large bowl.

Stir in egg and water.

Add ground beef and ground turkey. Mix well. Shape into 1 inch (2.5 cm) balls. Arrange in single layer on greased baking sheets with sides. Bake in 350°F (175°C) oven for 15 to 18 minutes. May be cooled, then frozen in single layer and placed in plastic bags or containers. Reheat from frozen state in 400°F (205°C) oven for 5 to 10 minutes until hot. Makes about 80.

1 coated meatball: 23 Calories; 1.1 g Total Fat; 64 mg Sodium; 2 g Protein; 1 g Carbohydrate; trace Dietary Fiber

Pictured on page 71.

PACIFIC RIBS

The thick brown sauce clings to the ribs. This one doesn't take much attention while cooking.

Pork spareribs, cut into short lengths (sweet and sour cut)	2 lbs.	900 g
Strained plums (baby food)	4½ oz.	128 mL
Apple cider vinegar	3 tbsp.	50 mL
Brown sugar, packed	½ cup	125 mL
Ketchup	3 tbsp.	50 mL
Ground ginger	1 tsp.	5 mL
Garlic powder	½ tsp.	2 mL
Salt	½ tsp.	2 mL
Pepper	⅛ tsp.	0.5 mL

Cut ribs apart into individual bones. Place in small roaster lined with greased foil.

Stir remaining 8 ingredients together in small bowl. Pour over ribs. Stir to coat. Cover. Bake in 350°F (175°C) oven for 2 hours, stirring every 20 to 30 minutes. Remove cover. Bake for 10 to 15 minutes. Drain. Makes about 40.

1 rib (with sauce): 42 Calories; 2 g Total Fat; 58 mg Sodium; 2 g Protein; 4 g Carbohydrate; trace Dietary Fiber

Pictured on page 71.

SWEET BACON DOGS

So easy and so good.

Wieners (1 lb., 454 g)	12	12
Thin bacon slices, each cut into 3 pieces	16	16
Brown sugar, packed	¼ cup	60 mL

Cut each wiener into 4 pieces. Wrap each piece with bacon, securing with wooden pick. Roll in brown sugar. Arrange in single layer on greased baking sheet or pan lined with greased foil. Sprinkle any remaining brown sugar over top. Bake in 250°F (120°C) oven for about 1½ hours. Serve warm. May be cooled and frozen. Reheat in 350°F (175°C) oven until bacon just begins to sizzle. Makes 48.

1 bacon dog: 47 Calories; 3.8 g Total Fat; 139 mg Sodium; 2 g Protein; 1 g Carbohydrate; trace Dietary Fiber

Pictured on page 107.

A different and satisfying way to serve ribs without the usual sweet, sticky sauce.

Pork spareribs	**2¼ lbs.**	**1 kg**
Water	**1 cup**	**250 mL**
White vinegar	**3 tbsp.**	**50 mL**
Soy sauce	**2 tbsp.**	**30 mL**
Salt	**1 tsp.**	**5 mL**
Pepper	**½ tsp.**	**2 mL**
Garlic powder	**½ tsp.**	**2 mL**
Bay leaves	**2**	**2**
Oyster sauce (optional)	**1 tbsp.**	**15 mL**

Cut meat between ribs to separate. Place in large saucepan.

Stir remaining 8 ingredients together in small bowl. Pour over ribs. Marinate for 1 hour in refrigerator, stirring often so top ribs are coated. Cover. Bring to a boil. Simmer for about 1 hour until tender. Discard bay leaves. Drain and reserve liquid. To serve, brush ribs with liquid. Arrange in single layer in baking pan lined with greased foil. Bake in 400°F (205°C) oven for 5 to 10 minutes until hot. Makes about 36.

1 rib (with sauce): 34 Calories; 2.5 g Total Fat; 142 mg Sodium; 3 g Protein; trace Carbohydrate; trace Dietary Fiber

Pictured on page 71.

Paré Pointer

You could quit your job due to illness and fatigue. You might be sick and tired of it.

YAKITORI

Little picks or skewers hold this delicious chicken. An attractive finger food.

Light-colored soy sauce	³/₄ cup	175 mL
Granulated sugar	¼ cup	60 mL
Sherry (or alcohol-free sherry)	¼ cup	60 mL
Garlic powder	¼ tsp.	1 mL
Pepper	⅛ tsp.	0.5 mL
Boneless, skinless chicken breast halves (about 1³/₄ lbs., 790 g), cut into 1 inch (2.5 cm) cubes	7	7
Medium green, red or yellow peppers, cut into 1 inch (2.5 cm) pieces to make about 30	2	2
Medium onions, cut into 1 inch (2.5 cm) pieces to make about 30	1-2	1-2

Combine first 5 ingredients in small saucepan. Stir. Bring to a boil over medium. Remove from heat.

Soak thirty 4 inch (10 cm) wooden skewers in water for 10 minutes. Thread each skewer with chicken, green pepper and onion. Place in hot sauce for 20 minutes. Spoon sauce over top several times during marinating. Remove from sauce. Arrange in single layer on greased broiler tray. Broil about 5 inches (12.5 cm) from heat for 2 minutes. Brush with sauce. Turn skewers over. Brush with sauce. Broil for 2 minutes. Repeat until chicken is cooked. Makes about 30.

1 kabob: 45 Calories; 0.4 g Total Fat; 454 mg Sodium; 7 g Protein; 3 g Carbohydrate; trace Dietary Fiber

Pictured on front cover.

PARTY WINGS

These have a sweet and sour taste with a rich brown glaze.

Apricot jam	½ cup	125 mL
Ketchup	⅓ cup	75 mL
Soy sauce	3 tbsp.	50 mL
Garlic powder	½ tsp.	2 mL
Whole chicken wings (or drumettes)	3 lbs.	1.4 kg

(continued on next page)

Mix first 4 ingredients in small bowl.

Remove wing tips and discard. Cut wings apart at joint. Arrange in single layer on greased baking sheet or pan lined with greased foil. Brush enough jam mixture over chicken to coat. Bake in 350°F (175°C) oven for 30 minutes. Brush with jam mixture. Bake for 10 minutes. Brush with remaining jam mixture. Bake for 10 minutes until tender. Makes about 36 wing pieces or 24 drumettes.

1 coated piece: 101 Calories; 6.1 g Total Fat; 147 mg Sodium; 7 g Protein; 4 g Carbohydrate; trace Dietary Fiber

Pictured on page 71.

BUFFALO WINGS

Another choice to make. Decide if you want hot wings or "suicide hot" wings.

Large eggs, fork-beaten	**2**	**2**
Milk	**¼ cup**	**60 mL**
Hot pepper sauce	**1 tbsp.**	**15 mL**
All-purpose flour	**⅔ cup**	**150 mL**
Seasoned salt	**2 tsp.**	**10 mL**
Pepper	**½ tsp.**	**2 mL**
Whole chicken wings (or drumettes)	**3 lbs.**	**1.4 kg**
Cooking oil, for deep-frying		
Commercial Louisiana Hot Sauce	**1-4 tbsp.**	**15-60 mL**

Combine eggs, milk and hot pepper sauce in small bowl.

Combine flour, seasoned salt and pepper in separate small bowl.

Remove wing tips and discard. Cut wings apart at joint. Dip a few pieces into egg mixture then into flour mixture to coat. Deep-fry in hot 375°F (190°C) cooking oil for 8 to 10 minutes until browned and crisp. Drain on paper towels. Put cooked chicken into large pail or bowl with cover.

Drizzle cooked chicken with hot sauce. Cover. Shake and toss for 1 to 2 minutes to distribute sauce evenly. Serve with Blue Cheese Dip, page 38. Makes about 36 wing pieces or 24 drumettes.

1 coated piece (with sauce): 108 Calories; 7.5 g Total Fat; 108 mg Sodium; 8 g Protein; 2 g Carbohydrate; trace Dietary Fiber

Pictured on page 107.

GLAZED MEATBALLS

So easy to cook these by simmering in a sauce. Dark brown glaze.

Lean ground beef	1½ lbs.	680 g
Envelope dry onion soup mix	1 × 1.4 oz.	1 × 38 g
Large egg	1	1
Ketchup	¼ cup	60 mL
Fine dry bread crumbs	⅓ cup	75 mL
Poultry seasoning, just a pinch		
Parsley flakes	¼ tsp.	1 mL
GLAZE		
Grape jelly	1½ cups	375 mL
Ketchup	¾ cup	175 mL
Lemon juice (or white vinegar), to taste (optional)		

Mix all 7 ingredients in medium bowl. Shape into 1 inch (2.5 cm) balls.

Glaze: Heat jelly and ketchup in frying pan until hot. Stir in lemon juice. Add meatballs. Stir gently to coat. Simmer, covered, for 20 to 25 minutes. Turn into chafing dish. Serve with wooden picks. Makes 60.

1 meatball (with glaze): 58 Calories; 1.9 g Total Fat; 134 mg Sodium; 3 g Protein; 8 g Carbohydrate; trace Dietary Fiber

Pictured on page 71.

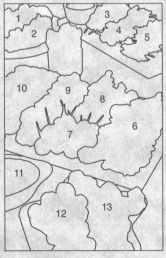

Props Courtesy Of: Stokes
The Bay

WIENER WISPS

Serve these wonderful morsels with picks. Sauce is thick and delectable.

Ketchup	½ cup	125 mL
Brown sugar, packed	½ cup	125 mL
Prepared mustard	1 tsp.	5 mL
Onion powder	¼ tsp.	1 mL
Rum flavoring	½ tsp.	2 mL
Water	½ cup	125 mL
Wieners (about 1 lb., 454 g), each cut into 6 pieces	12	12

Measure first 6 ingredients into medium saucepan. Stir.

Add wiener pieces. Bring to a boil. Cover. Simmer for about 15 minutes. Serve hot in chafing dish. Makes 72.

1 piece (with sauce): 28 Calories; 1.8 g Total Fat; 95 mg Sodium; 1 g Protein; 2 g Carbohydrate; trace Dietary Fiber

Pictured on page 17.

SAUCY GARLIC SAUSAGE: Rather than wieners, slice garlic sausage into sauce. Excellent.

POLYNESIAN SAUSAGES

These are outstanding. Coated with a sweet and tangy sauce.

Apricot jam	1 cup	250 mL
Apple cider vinegar	3 tbsp.	50 mL
Paprika	¼ tsp.	1 mL
Onion powder	¼ tsp.	1 mL
Parsley flakes	¼ tsp.	1 mL
Garlic powder	¼ tsp.	1 mL
Salami cocktail sausages, cooked	1 lb.	454 g

Measure first 6 ingredients into 3½ quart (3.5 L) slow cooker. Stir well.

Add sausages. Stir. Cover. Cook on Low for 2 to 4 hours or on High for 1 to 2 hours until heated through. Serve with wooden picks. Makes about 22.

1 sausage (with sauce): 100 Calories; 5.2 g Total Fat; 199 mg Sodium; 2 g Protein; 11 g Carbohydrate; trace Dietary Fiber

SIMPLE MEATBALLS

These are extra good on their own, or serve with Simple Sweet And Sour Sauce, page 41. The sauce can be served as a dip beside the meatballs or can be poured over them.

Fine dry bread crumbs	½ cup	125 mL
Finely minced onion	¼ cup	60 mL
Water	⅓ cup	75 mL
Prepared horseradish	1 tsp.	5 mL
Salt	1 tsp.	5 mL
Pepper	¼ tsp.	1 mL
Lean ground beef	1 lb.	454 g

Stir first 6 ingredients together well in medium bowl.

Add ground beef. Mix well. Shape into 1 inch (2.5 cm) balls. Arrange in single layer on greased baking sheet or pan. Bake in 375°F (190°C) oven for about 15 minutes until no longer pink. Drain. Makes 40.

1 meatball (with sauce): 23 Calories; 1 g Total Fat; 83 mg Sodium; 2 g Protein; 1 g Carbohydrate; trace Dietary Fiber

TORTILLA STACKS

Easy to serve on small plates in the living room before the call to the table. Delicious.

Lean ground beef	½ lb.	225 g
Finely chopped onion	½ cup	125 mL
Picante salsa	3 tbsp.	50 mL
Flour tortillas (10 inch, 25 cm, size)	3	3
Canned diced green chilies, drained	4 oz.	114 mL
Medium tomato, seeded and diced	1	1
Grated Monterey Jack cheese	⅓ cup	75 mL
Grated medium Cheddar cheese	⅓ cup	75 mL

(continued on next page)

Scramble-fry ground beef and onion in non-stick frying pan until beef is no longer pink and onion is soft. Drain well.

Stir in salsa. Cool.

Lay 1 tortilla on greased baking sheet. Spread meat sauce over top to edge. Cover with second tortilla. Sprinkle with green chilies. Top with third tortilla. Scatter tomato over tortilla.

Toss both cheeses together. Sprinkle over top. Bake in 425°F (220°C) oven for about 15 minutes. Cuts into 8 wedges.

1 wedge: 155 Calories; 5.8 g Total Fat; 318 mg Sodium; 10 g Protein; 15 g Carbohydrate; 1 g Dietary Fiber

GLAZED HAM CANAPÉS

An appetizer with sustenance. Especially good when serving an appetizer meal.

Canned cola-flavored beverage	1 × 12½ oz.	1 × 355 mL
Apricot (or peach) jam	¼ cup	60 mL
Ground cloves	¼ tsp.	1 mL
Cooked smoked ham	1½ lbs.	680 g
Small butter crackers (such as Ritz)	48	48
Prepared mustard	3 tbsp.	50 mL

Stir first 3 ingredients in ungreased 2 quart (2 L) casserole.

Set ham in cola mixture. Cover. Bake in 325°F (160°) oven for 2 hours, turning ham several times. Cool. Chill until needed.

Serve thin slices, cut to fit, over crackers that have been spread with a little prepared mustard. Makes 48.

1 canapé: 46 Calories; 1.8 g Total Fat; 427 mg Sodium; 4 g Protein; 3 g Carbohydrate; trace Dietary Fiber

Paré Pointer

You get a hangover by eating too much.

WIENER BITES

Tart, sweet sauce that complements the wiener pieces. Serve hot with picks.

Black currant (or blackberry) jelly	**1¼ cups**	**300 mL**
Prepared mustard	**½ cup**	**125 mL**
Wieners (1 lb., 454 g), each cut into 6 pieces	**12**	**12**

Heat jelly and mustard in large saucepan.

Add wiener pieces. Cover. Simmer, stirring often, until wiener pieces are puffed. Serve with wooden picks. Makes about 72.

1 piece (with sauce): 37 Calories; 1.9 g Total Fat; 94 mg Sodium; 1 g Protein; 4 g Carbohydrate; trace Dietary Fiber

COCKTAIL SAUSAGES

A bit sweet and a bit tangy.

Grape jelly	**1 cup**	**250 mL**
Chili sauce	**1 cup**	**250 mL**
Lemon juice	**1 tsp.**	**5 mL**
Frozen concentrated orange juice	**3 tbsp.**	**50 mL**
Salami cocktail sausages, cooked	**2 lbs.**	**900 g**

Combine first 4 ingredients in 3½ quart (3.5 L) slow cooker. Stir well.

Add sausages. Stir gently. Cover. Cook on Low for 4 to 5 hours or on High for 2 to 2½ hours until hot. Makes 44.

1 sausage (with sauce): 107 Calories; 5.8 g Total Fat; 346 mg Sodium; 3 g Protein; 11 g Carbohydrate; 1 g Dietary Fiber

Paré Pointer

You know a mummy has a cold when it starts coffin.

BEEF SKEWERS

Once these marinated and broiled appetizers show up, they are gone in a flash. Can be prepared on skewers, chilled and broiled at the last minute.

Light soy sauce	²/₃ cup	150 mL
Lemon juice	1 tbsp.	15 mL
White vinegar	1 tbsp.	15 mL
Brown sugar, packed	¼ cup	60 mL
Ground ginger	1 tsp.	5 mL
Garlic powder	¼ tsp.	1 mL
Onion powder	¼ tsp.	1 mL
Pepper	¼ tsp.	1 mL
Beef sirloin steak, cut into ¾ inch (2 cm) cubes	1½ lbs.	680 g

Mix first 8 ingredients in medium bowl with tight fitting cover.

Add steak cubes. Stir. Cover tightly. Marinate in refrigerator for 6 to 8 hours or overnight. Flip bowl or stir cubes occasionally. Soak thirty 4 inch (10 cm) wooden skewers in water for 10 minutes. Remove meat from marinade with slotted spoon. Discard marinade. Thread 3 cubes on each skewer. Place on greased broiling tray. Broil 4 inches (10 cm) from heat for 4 to 8 minutes, turning as needed, until desired doneness. Makes about 30.

1 kabob: 24 Calories; 0.8 g Total Fat; 56 mg Sodium; 4 g Protein; trace Carbohydrate; 0 g Dietary Fiber

Paré Pointer

He just swallowed a bone. He's not choking—he's serious.

STUFFED MUSHROOMS

A bit gooey and a real hit.

Fresh medium mushrooms	36	36
Pork sausage meat	½ lb.	225 g
All-purpose flour	1 tbsp.	15 mL
Fine dry bread crumbs	¼ cup	60 mL
Picante salsa	¼ cup	60 mL
Process mozzarella cheese slices, each cut into 12 smaller squares	3	3

Carefully twist stems from mushrooms. Chop stems.

Scramble-fry sausage meat and mushroom stems until no pink remains in sausage. Drain.

Sprinkle flour over sausage meat mixture. Mix. Add bread crumbs. Stir. Stir in salsa until mixture comes to a boil. Remove from heat. Stuff mushroom caps. Arrange in single layer on ungreased baking sheet.

Place cheese square over top of each. Bake in 400°F (205°C) oven for about 12 minutes. Serve warm. Makes 36.

1 stuffed mushroom: 27 Calories; 1.6 g Total Fat; 85 mg Sodium; 1 g Protein; 2 g Carbohydrate; trace Dietary Fiber

Pictured on page 17.

STUFFED PEA PODS

Cute and colorful. Different from the usual stuffed pea pods.

Fresh pea pods	24	24
Boiling water, to cover		
Canned ham flakes, drained	6½ oz.	184 g
Salad dressing (or mayonnaise)	1 tbsp.	15 mL
Sweet pickle relish	1½ tsp.	7 mL
Prepared mustard	¼ tsp.	1 mL
Chopped chives	2 tsp.	10 mL

(continued on next page)

Put pea pods into medium bowl. Pour boiling water over to cover well. Let stand for 1 minute. Drain. Rinse in cold water until cooled. Drain. Slit top sides (least curved sides) open.

Mash remaining 5 ingredients with fork in small bowl. Makes 1 cup (250 mL) filling. Stuff each pea pod with about 2 tsp. (10 mL) filling. Makes 24.

1 stuffed pea pod: 24 Calories; 1.8 g Total Fat; 111 mg Sodium; 1 g Protein; 1 g Carbohydrate; trace Dietary Fiber

Pictured on page 89.

SNACKIN' POTATO SKINS

Always a favorite. Seasoned and crisp. Serve with sour cream and chopped green onion on the side.

Medium baking potatoes, baked and cooled	**5**	**5**
Hard margarine (or butter), melted	**¼ cup**	**60 mL**
Seasoned salt, sprinkle		

Cut potatoes in half lengthwise. Cut each half lengthwise. Now cut all 20 strips in half crosswise making 40 pieces. Scoop away most of the potato leaving a thin layer on each skin.

Brush both sides with margarine. Sprinkle with seasoned salt. Place, skin side up, on ungreased baking sheet. Bake in 400°F (205°C) oven for 10 to 15 minutes until crisp. Makes 40 pieces.

1 coated potato skin: 24 Calories; 1.1 g Total Fat; 15 mg Sodium; trace Protein; 3 g Carbohydrate; trace Dietary Fiber

Variation #1: Omit seasoned salt. Sprinkle with ½ envelope of taco seasoning. Bake as above. Serve with Guacamole, page 32.

Pictured on page 17.

Variation #2: Omit margarine and seasoned salt. Place potato wedges, skin side down, on ungreased baking sheet. Sprinkle with 1 cup (250 mL) grated Cheddar cheese. Add either ⅓ cup (75 mL) cooked and crumbled bacon or ⅓ cup (75 mL) chopped green onion, or a combination of both. Bake as above.

Pictured on page 17.

PRIZE MUSHROOMS

Attractive and so different.

Large fresh portobello mushrooms, 5-6 inches (12.5-15 cm) in diameter	6	6
Cooking oil	2 tsp.	10 mL
Hard margarine (or butter)	1 tsp.	5 mL
Garlic clove, minced (or ¼ tsp., 1 mL, garlic powder)	1	1
Chopped onion	1 cup	250 mL
Finely chopped red pepper	2 tbsp.	30 mL
Salt	¼ tsp.	1 mL
Pepper, sprinkle		
Grated part-skim mozzarella cheese	1 cup	250 mL
Chopped chives	1 tbsp.	15 mL
Grated Parmesan cheese	1 tbsp.	15 mL

Remove stems from mushrooms. Brush both sides of caps with cooking oil. Arrange in single layer on ungreased baking sheet. Broil both sides, about 6 inches (15 cm) from heat for 4 to 5 minutes per side until caps begin to soften.

Heat margarine in frying pan. Add garlic, onion and red pepper. Sprinkle with salt and pepper. Sauté until golden. Divide and spoon into mushroom caps.

Divide and layer remaining 3 ingredients over onion mixture in each cap. Broil until cheese is melted and nicely browned. Makes 6 servings.

1 stuffed mushroom: 118 Calories; 7.4 g Total Fat; 255 mg Sodium; 7 g Protein; 7 g Carbohydrate; 1 g Dietary Fiber

Pictured on page 143.

CARROT CURLS

A colorful, crisp and easy addition to salads or to a raw vegetable platter with dip.

Large carrots	2	2
Cold water, to cover		

(continued on next page)

Peel carrots lengthwise into wide strips using vegetable peeler.

Curl each carrot strip around finger. Fasten with wooden pick. Place in large bowl filled with enough water to cover all curls. Chill for at least 2 hours. Drain. Set curls on paper towels. Remove wooden picks just before placing on salad or on tray. Makes about 16.

1 carrot curl: 5 Calories; trace Total Fat; 4 mg Sodium; trace Protein; 1 g Carbohydrate; trace Dietary Fiber

Pictured on page 89.

MYSTERY APPETIZER

A real conversation item. Have friends guess what it is.

Fine dry bread crumbs	2/3 cup	150 mL
Grated Parmesan cheese	1/2 cup	125 mL
Parsley flakes	1/2 tsp.	2 mL
Poultry seasoning	1/4 tsp.	1 mL
Onion powder	1/4 tsp.	1 mL
Salt	1/16 tsp.	0.5 mL
Pepper, just a pinch		
Large eggplant, peeled and cut like french fries	1	1
Salad dressing (or mayonnaise)	2/3 cup	150 mL

Stir first 7 ingredients together in small bowl.

Dip eggplant pieces into salad dressing to coat. Roll in crumb mixture. Arrange in single layer on greased baking sheet. Bake in 400°F (205°C) oven for about 12 minutes until browned. Serve immediately as eggplant tends to darken upon standing. Makes about 60.

1 coated "fry": 24 Calories; 1.7 g Total Fat; 46 mg Sodium; 1 g Protein; 2 g Carbohydrate; trace Dietary Fiber

Pictured on page 107.

Paré Pointer

Honey is very scarce in Thailand. Bangkok has only one "B."

MARINATED VEGETABLES

A bright and colorful addition to a tray of starters.

Cooking oil	½ cup	125 mL
Lemon juice	2 tbsp.	30 mL
White vinegar	2 tbsp.	30 mL
Granulated sugar	1½ tsp.	7 mL
Salt	½ tsp.	2 mL
Dry mustard	¼ tsp.	1 mL
Onion salt	¼ tsp.	1 mL
Paprika	¼ tsp.	1 mL
Dried whole oregano	¼ tsp.	1 mL
Garlic salt	¼ tsp.	1 mL
Ground thyme	¹⁄₁₆ tsp.	0.5 mL
Cauliflower florets	1½ cups	375 mL
Broccoli florets	1½ cups	375 mL
Small fresh mushrooms	1 cup	250 mL
Medium green pepper, cut into strips	1	1
Cherry tomatoes	1½ cups	375 mL
Diagonally sliced celery	1 cup	250 mL
Medium carrot, cut into sticks	1	1

Stir first 11 ingredients together well in large bowl with tight fitting lid. Makes ¾ cup (175 mL) marinade.

Add remaining 7 ingredients. Cover. Turn over to coat vegetables. Chill for several hours or overnight, turning or shaking bowl occasionally. Serve in marinade with slotted spoon. Makes 8 cups (2 L).

¼ cup (60 mL): 23 Calories; 1.9 g Total Fat; 39 mg Sodium; trace Protein; 2 g Carbohydrate; trace Dietary Fiber

Pictured on page 89.

Paré Pointer

When asked if he'd lived here all his life, he replied, "Not yet."

SAVORY PALMIERS

Cute little treats that will please everyone. Real showstoppers, but not hard to make at all. This version is without the sugar.

Cooking oil	2 tsp.	10 mL
Finely chopped onion	1 cup	250 mL
Finely chopped fresh mushrooms	2 cups	500 mL
Hard margarine (or butter)	1 tsp.	5 mL
All-purpose flour	4 tsp.	20 mL
Salt	1/4 tsp.	1 mL
Pepper	1/16 tsp.	0.5 mL
Garlic powder	1/4 tsp.	1 mL
Light sour cream	1/4 cup	60 mL
Frozen puff pastry, thawed according to package directions	1/2 x 14.1 oz.	1/2 x 397 g

Heat cooking oil in frying pan. Add onion. Sauté until soft. Blot onions on paper towel. Spoon into small bowl.

Add mushrooms and margarine to frying pan. Sauté until golden. Add onion to mushrooms.

Sprinkle with flour, salt, pepper and garlic powder. Mix well.

Stir in sour cream until mixture is boiling and thickened. Cool.

Roll out pastry on lightly floured surface to rectangle measuring 11 x 13 inches (28 x 33 cm). Cut lengthwise, down center, forming 2 long rectangles. Spread 1/2 of mushroom mixture over surface, leaving 1/2 inch (12 mm) space down each side. Roll each long side to meet in center just touching each other. Dampen pastry along each edge. Press together lightly. Wrap in plastic wrap. Chill for 30 to 40 minutes.

Cut each chilled roll into 24 slices, each slice about 1/2 inch (12 mm) wide. Arrange on greased baking sheet, cut side down. Bake in upper third of 375°F (190°C) oven for about 12 minutes until golden. Serve warm. Makes 48.

1 palmier: 26 Calories; 1.7 g Total Fat; 39 mg Sodium; trace Protein; 2 g Carbohydrate; trace Dietary Fiber

Pictured on page 89.

IMPOSSIBLE BACON QUICHE

This makes its own crust while baking. Nice flavor of bacon and onion.

Bacon slices, cooked crisp and crumbled	12-15	12-15
Shredded Swiss cheese	1 cup	250 mL
Finely chopped onion	¼ cup	60 mL
Milk	2 cups	500 mL
Biscuit mix	1 cup	250 mL
Large eggs	4	4
Salt	¼ tsp.	1 mL
Pepper	⅛ tsp.	0.5 mL

Grease 10 inch (25 cm) pie plate. Sprinkle bacon over bottom. Scatter cheese over bacon. Scatter onion over cheese.

Put milk, biscuit mix, eggs, salt and pepper into blender or medium bowl. Process or beat together well. Pour into pie plate. Bake in 400°F (205°C) oven for about 35 minutes until knife inserted near center comes out clean. Cuts into 10 wedges for a sit-down appetizer.

1 wedge: 197 Calories; 11.1 g Total Fat; 446 mg Sodium; 11 g Protein; 13 g Carbohydrate; trace Dietary Fiber

CHEESE TARTS

A winner every time.

Grated medium Cheddar cheese	½ cup	125 mL
Grated Havarti (or other white) cheese	½ cup	125 mL
Chopped onion	1 tbsp.	15 mL
Salt	¼ tsp.	1 mL
Pepper, just a pinch		
Dry mustard, just a pinch		
Large egg	1	1
Milk	½ cup	125 mL
Unbaked mini-tart shells	24	24

Measure first 8 ingredients into blender. Process until smooth.

Pour into tart shells. Bake in 350°F (175°C) oven for 20 to 25 minutes until set. Makes 24.

1 tart: 59 Calories; 4.1 g Total Fat; 111 mg Sodium; 2 g Protein; 3 g Carbohydrate; trace Dietary Fiber

PHYLLO NESTS

Very pretty. Ready for the filling of your choice.

Frozen phyllo pastry sheets, thawed according to package directions	3	3
Hard margarine (or butter), melted	2 tbsp.	30 mL

Lay 1 pastry sheet on working surface. Working quickly, brush with melted margarine. Cover with second sheet. Brush with melted margarine. Repeat with remaining sheet. Cut layered strip into 2½ inch (6.4 cm) squares. Carefully press into greased mini-muffin pans. Bake in 375°F (190°C) oven for 5 to 6 minutes until browned. Let stand for 5 minutes before removing to rack to cool. Makes 20.

1 unfilled nest: 21 Calories; 1.2 g Total Fat; 33 mg Sodium; trace Protein; 2 g Carbohydrate; trace Dietary Fiber

Pictured on front cover.

PIQUANT BEEF FILLING

The dark meaty filling complements the light-colored pastry.

Lean ground beef	½ lb.	225 g
Finely chopped onion	¼ cup	60 mL
All-purpose flour	1 tbsp.	15 mL
Salt	¼ tsp.	1 mL
Pepper, sprinkle		
Soy sauce	1 tbsp.	15 mL
Milk	⅓ cup	75 mL

Scramble-fry ground beef and onion in non-stick frying pan until no pink remains in meat and onion is soft.

Sprinkle with flour, salt and pepper. Mix well.

Stir in soy sauce and milk until boiling. Remove from heat. Chill until needed. Reheat filling just before serving. Serve in Toast Cups, page 14, or Phyllo Nests, above. Makes 1⅓ cups (325 mL).

1 tbsp. (15 mL): 26 Calories; 1.6 g Total Fat; 86 mg Sodium; 2 g Protein; 1 g Carbohydrate; trace Dietary Fiber

Pictured on front cover.

MUSHROOM PASTRIES

Pass these lavish pastries and watch them disappear.

CREAM CHEESE PASTRY

Cream cheese, softened	4 oz.	125 g
Hard margarine (or butter), softened	½ cup	125 mL
All-purpose flour	1½ cups	375 mL

MUSHROOM FILLING

Hard margarine (or butter)	2 tbsp.	30 mL
Chopped onion	1 cup	250 mL
Fresh mushrooms, chopped	½ lb.	225 g
All-purpose flour	2 tbsp.	30 mL
Salt	1 tsp.	5 mL
Pepper	¼ tsp.	1 mL
Ground thyme	¼ tsp.	1 mL
Salad dressing (or mayonnaise)	⅓ cup	75 mL
Worcestershire sauce	¼ tsp.	1 mL
Large egg, fork-beaten	1	1

Cream Cheese Pastry: Beat cream cheese and margarine together well in medium bowl. Work in flour until a ball is formed. Chill for at least 1 hour.

Mushroom Filling: Melt margarine in frying pan. Add onion and mushrooms. Sauté until soft.

Add flour, salt, pepper and thyme. Stir well.

Add salad dressing and Worcestershire sauce. Stir until mixture is boiling and thickened. Remove from heat. Cool well.

Roll out pastry on lightly floured surface. Cut into thirty-six 2 inch (5 cm) circles using a scalloped edge if possible. Place 1 tsp. (5 mL) filling in center of 18 circles. Moisten edges with egg. Cover with remaining pastry circles. Seal edges with fork. Cut 2 or 3 slits in top of each. Arrange on ungreased baking sheet. Bake in 425°F (220°C) oven for about 10 minutes until browned. Makes 36.

1 pastry: 81 Calories; 5.9 g Total Fat; 142 mg Sodium; 1 g Protein; 6 g Carbohydrate; trace Dietary Fiber

SPICY SAUSAGE ROLLS

An all-beef make-yourself sausage. Spicy but not too hot.

Dry bread crumbs	½ cup	125 mL
Water	¼ cup	60 mL
White vinegar	2 tbsp.	30 mL
Chili powder	2 tsp.	10 mL
Salt	1 tsp.	5 mL
Pepper	¼ tsp.	1 mL
Dried whole oregano	½ tsp.	2 mL
Garlic powder	¼ tsp.	1 mL
Worcestershire sauce	½ tsp.	2 mL
Lean ground beef	1 lb.	454 g

**Pastry, your own or a mix, enough
for 3 crusts**

Stir first 9 ingredients in medium bowl. Add ground beef. Mix well. Roll into 3½ inch (9 cm) lengths, size of a small sausage in roundness.

Roll out ⅓ of pastry on lightly floured surface into. Place 1 beef sausage on outer edge. Cut strip width of sausage. Roll up just enough to allow a bit of overlap. Cut to separate from pastry. Moisten overlap to seal. Cut roll in half. Place on ungreased baking tray. Continue until all sausages and pastry are rolled. Bake in 400°F (205°C) oven for 20 to 25 minutes until browned. Serve immediately or cool. Chill or freeze. To reheat, bake in 400°F (205°C) oven for 5 to 10 minutes until hot. Makes about 46.

1 roll: 86 Calories; 5.5 g Total Fat; 148 mg Sodium; 3 g Protein; 6 g Carbohydrate; trace Dietary Fiber

SAUSAGE ROLLS: Precook skinless sausages in frying pan until half cooked. Cool. Roll in pastry as above.

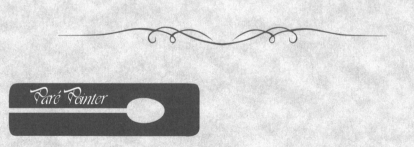

Paré Pointer

Peanuts must be very fattening. Have you ever seen a skinny elephant?

MINI CREAM PUFF SHELLS

A versatile marvel. Fill with hot or cold fillings. You can hide a filling completely or serve these bulging.

Water	**1 cup**	**250 mL**
Hard margarine (or butter)	**½ cup**	**125 mL**
Salt	**¼ tsp.**	**1 mL**
All-purpose flour	**1 cup**	**250 mL**
Large eggs	**4**	**4**

Combine water, margarine and salt in medium saucepan. Bring to a boil over medium.

Add flour. Stir until mixture leaves sides of pan and clumps together. Remove from heat.

Beat in eggs, 1 at a time, beating well after each addition. Drop small spoonfuls onto ungreased baking sheet, leaving room for expansion. Bake in 400°F (205°C) oven for about 15 minutes until puffed and browned. They should look dry. Cool on rack. Cut tops almost, or completely, off. Fill shells. Replace tops. Makes about 72 one-bite size or 36 two-bite size.

1 one-bite size: 23 Calories; 1.7 g Total Fat; 29 mg Sodium; 1 g Protein; 1 g Carbohydrate; trace Dietary Fiber

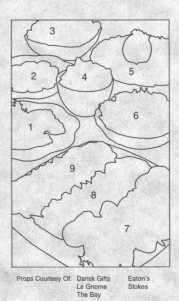

1. Mozza Pepper Toast, page 9
2. Savory Palmiers, page 83
3. Marinated Vegetables, page 82
4. Little Smokies, page 61
5. Bruschetta Pizza, page 19
6. Veggie Chips, page 112
7. Carrot Curls, page 80
8. Stuffed Pea Pods, page 78
9. Marinated Shrimp, page 56

Props Courtesy Of: Dansk Gifts   Eaton's
                    Le Gnome   Stokes
                    The Bay

Mild mustard and orange flavors, with a touch of sweetness.

Canned ham flakes, drained	**6¹/₂ oz.**	**184 g**
Brown sugar, packed	**1 tbsp.**	**15 mL**
Dry mustard	**1 tbsp.**	**15 mL**
Water	**1¹/₂ tsp.**	**7 mL**
Finely grated orange peel (or 1 tbsp., 15 mL, orange marmalade)	**¹/₈ tsp.**	**0.5 mL**
Pastry, your own or a mix, enough for 2 crusts		
Large egg, fork-beaten	**1**	**1**

Mash first 5 ingredients together well on large plate.

Roll out pastry on lightly floured surface. Cut into 3 inch (7.5 cm) squares. Place 1¹/₂ tsp. (7 mL) ham mixture in center. Moisten edges of pastry with water. Fold over, pressing with fork to seal. Cut tiny slits in tops. Arrange on ungreased baking sheet.

Brush with egg. Bake in 400°F (205°C) oven for about 15 minutes until lightly browned. Serve immediately or freeze in single layer on baking sheet then place in container. To reheat, arrange on ungreased baking sheet. Heat in 350°F (175°C) oven for 20 to 25 minutes until hot and pastry is crispy. Makes 20.

***1 turnover:** 121 Calories; 8.2 g Total Fat; 239 mg Sodium; 3 g Protein; 9 g Carbohydrate; trace Dietary Fiber*

Pictured on page 53.

Paré Pointer

Robin Hood robbed the rich because the poor didn't have any money.

PARTY QUICHE

To make these look as good as they taste, garnish with a few shreds of cheese or a dab of sour cream. Excellent.

Grated medium Cheddar (or Swiss) cheese	1 cup	250 mL
Milk	½ cup	125 mL
Large egg	1	1
Sliced fresh mushrooms	1 cup	250 mL
Salt	¼ tsp.	1 mL
Real bacon bits (or 6 slices bacon, cooked crisp and crumbled)	½ cup	125 mL
Unbaked mini-tart shells	24	24

Place first 5 ingredients in blender. Process until smooth.

Divide bacon bits among tart shells. Spoon cheese mixture over bacon. Bake in 350°F (175°C) oven for about 25 minutes until set. Makes 24.

1 quiche: 70 Calories; 5 g Total Fat; 133 mg Sodium; 3 g Protein; 4 g Carbohydrate; trace Dietary Fiber

HAM FILLING

Makes a mellow, flavorful filling or may also be served as a dip with crackers or chips.

Canned ham flakes, drained	6½ oz.	184 g
Salad dressing (or mayonnaise)	¼ cup	60 mL
Sour cream	¼ cup	60 mL
Green onions, chopped	2	2
Prepared mustard	1 tsp.	5 mL
Prepared horseradish	1 tsp.	5 mL
Lemon juice	½ tsp.	2 mL
Pepper	¹⁄₁₆ tsp.	0.5 mL

Mix all 8 ingredients well in small bowl. Chill until needed. Serve in Toast Cups, page 14, or Phyllo Nests, page 85. Makes 1⅓ cups (325 mL).

1 tbsp. (15 mL): 39 Calories; 3.3 g Total Fat; 136 mg Sodium; 1 g Protein; 1 g Carbohydrate; trace Dietary Fiber

Pictured on front cover.

Good hot or cold. Fancy.

Large egg	1	1
Cream cheese, softened	4 oz.	125 g
Feta cheese, crumbled	8 oz.	250 g
Grated Parmesan cheese	2 tbsp.	30 mL
Parsley flakes	1 tsp.	5 mL
Frozen phyllo pastry sheets (about 1 lb., 454 g), thawed according to package directions	16	16
Hard margarine (or butter), melted	1 cup	250 mL

Beat egg in small bowl until frothy. Add all 3 cheeses and parsley. Beat until smooth.

Lay 1 pastry sheet on working surface. Cover remaining pastry with damp tea towel. Working quickly, brush sheet generously with melted margarine. ❶ Cut into four 4 inch (10 cm) wide strips, along longer edge. ❷ Fold each strip in half lengthwise to make 2 inch (5 cm) wide strips. Brush with margarine. ❸ Place 1 tsp. (5 cm) cheese mixture in center at 1 end. ❹ Fold 1 corner over to form triangle ❺ Continue folding over in same fashion to end of strip. Brush final triangle with margarine. Place on ungreased baking sheet. Repeat with remaining cheese mixture and pastry sheets. Bake in 400°F (205°C) oven for about 15 minutes until golden. Makes 64.

1 triangle: 65 Calories; 4.5 g Total Fat; 126 mg Sodium; 1 g Protein; 5 g Carbohydrate; trace Dietary Fiber

Pictured on page 53.

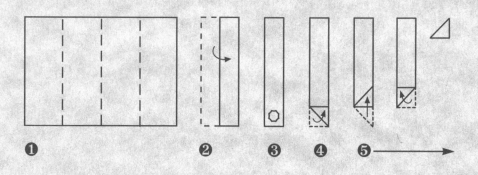

MUSHROOM TARTS

This filling can be prepared ahead along with baking the tart shells ahead too. Freezes well. Good mushroom flavor.

Hard margarine (or butter)	1 tbsp.	15 mL
Chopped fresh mushrooms	1 cup	250 mL
Chopped green onion	1 tbsp.	15 mL
All-purpose flour	2 tbsp.	30 mL
Salt	¼ tsp.	1 mL
Skim evaporated milk (or light cream)	⅔ cup	150 mL
Unbaked mini-tart shells	18	18

Melt margarine in medium saucepan. Add mushrooms and green onion. Sauté until golden.

Mix in flour and salt.

Add evaporated milk, stirring until boiling and thickened. Cool. Makes generous 1 cup (250 mL) filling.

Bake unfilled tart shells in 400°F (205°C) oven for 10 to 13 minutes until lightly browned. Cool. Divide mushroom mixture evenly among tart shells. Bake in 400°F (205°C) oven for 5 minutes until hot. To heat from frozen state allow about 10 minutes. Makes 18.

1 tart: 53 Calories; 3 g Total Fat; 100 mg Sodium; 1 g Protein; 5 g Carbohydrate; trace Dietary Fiber

BEEFY ROLL-UPS

An attractive pinwheel effect with dark beef and orange cheese. Tasty and easy.

Light cream cheese, softened	4 oz.	125 g
Sour cream	¼ cup	60 mL
Prepared horseradish, more or less	1½ tsp.	7 mL
Prepared mustard	1 tsp.	5 mL
Chopped chives	2 tsp.	10 mL
Flour tortillas (8 inch, 20 cm, size)	4	4
Shaved deli beef	8 oz.	225 g
Grated medium Cheddar cheese	1¼ cups	300 mL

(continued on next page)

Mix first 5 ingredients well in small bowl.

Divide and spread over each tortilla.

Lay beef over top. Sprinkle with cheese. Roll each up as tightly as possible. Wrap in plastic wrap. Chill for at least 1 hour. Trim ends. Cut each roll into 10 slices, for a total of 40.

1 slice: *42 Calories; 2.2 g Total Fat; 163 mg Sodium; 3 g Protein; 2 g Carbohydrate; trace Dietary Fiber*

Pictured on page 17.

TORTILLA ROLL-UPS

So attractive in colorful tortillas.

Cream cheese, softened	**8 oz.**	**250 g**
Salad dressing (or mayonnaise)	**¼ cup**	**60 mL**
Envelope ranch-style salad dressing mix (stir before dividing)	**½ × 1 oz.**	**½ × 28 g**
Finely chopped green onion	**¼ cup**	**60 mL**
Canned diced green chilies, drained and patted dry with paper towels	**4 oz.**	**114 mL**
Chopped pimiento, drained and patted dry with paper towels	**2 oz.**	**57 mL**
Plain (or dried tomato or pesto) flour tortillas (10 inch, 25 cm, size)	**8**	**8**

Beat cream cheese and salad dressing in medium bowl until smooth.

Stir in next 4 ingredients.

Spread ¼ cup (60 mL) creamy mixture on each tortilla right to edge. Roll up snugly. Chill for at least 2 hours. Trim ends. Cut each roll into 8 slices, for a total of 64.

1 slice: *32 Calories; 1.1 g Total Fat; 63 mg Sodium; 1 g Protein; 5 g Carbohydrate; trace Dietary Fiber*

Pictured on page 35.

Paré Pointer

Saleswoman at perfume counter to customer: "If this stuff really worked, would I be standing here eight hours a day?"

SALAD ROLLS

See-through rice paper wrappers. These can be picked up with fingers.

Apple cider vinegar	2 tbsp.	30 mL
Lemon juice	1 tbsp.	15 mL
Brown sugar, packed	3 tbsp.	50 mL
Plum sauce	3 tbsp.	50 mL
Soy sauce	1 tbsp.	15 mL
Hoisin sauce	1 tbsp.	15 mL
Grated gingerroot	$\frac{1}{2}$ tsp.	2 mL
Cornstarch	1 tsp.	5 mL
Dried crushed chilies	$\frac{1}{8}$-$\frac{1}{4}$ tsp.	0.5-1 mL
Shredded fresh spinach, packed	$1\frac{1}{2}$ cups	375 mL
Chopped fresh bean sprouts	$1\frac{1}{2}$ cups	375 mL
Thinly sliced fresh mushrooms	$\frac{2}{3}$ cup	150 mL
Grated carrot	$\frac{1}{2}$ cup	125 mL
Finely sliced red onion	$\frac{1}{4}$ cup	60 mL
Rice papers (8$\frac{1}{2}$ inch, 21.5 cm, size)	20	20
Hot water		

Chopped peanuts, for garnish (optional)

Combine first 9 ingredients in small saucepan. Heat and stir until boiling. Cool.

Combine next 5 ingredients in medium bowl. Add cooled vinegar mixture. Toss.

Soak 1 sheet of rice paper in hot water in shallow dish for about 1 minute until soft and pliable. If left too long it will become very fragile. ❶ Place about 2 tbsp. (30 mL) filling in 3 inch (7.5 cm) row off center of rice paper. ❷ Fold 1 end up and over filling, tucking under. ❸ Fold both sides over. ❹ Roll up snugly. Repeat with remaining rice papers and filling.

Garnish with peanuts. Serve immediately. Do not refrigerate. Makes 20.

1 roll: 60 Calories; 0.2 g Total Fat; 102 mg Sodium; 1 g Protein; 14 g Carbohydrate; 1 g Dietary Fiber

Pictured on page 125.

(continued on next page)

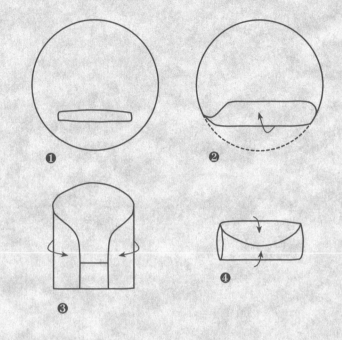

CHEESY ROLL-UPS

Basically white in color with green onion and green chilies showing in the pinwheel design.

Cream cheese, softened	4 oz.	125 g
Sour cream	½ cup	125 mL
Finely chopped green onion	¼ cup	60 mL
Canned diced green chilies, drained	4 oz.	114 mL
Seasoned salt	¼ tsp.	1 mL
Garlic powder	⅛ tsp.	0.5 mL
Flour tortillas (8 inch, 20 cm, size)	6	6

Beat cream cheese and sour cream together in small bowl until smooth.

Add next 4 ingredients. Stir. Makes 1½ cups (375 mL).

Spread each tortilla to edge with ¼ cup (60 mL) mixture. Roll up snugly, like jelly roll. Wrap in plastic wrap. Chill for at least 2 hours. Trim ends. Cut each roll into 10 slices, for a total of 60.

1 slice: 22 Calories; 1.1 g Total Fat; 38 mg Sodium; 1 g Protein; 2 g Carbohydrate; trace Dietary Fiber

Pictured on page 35.

ORIENTAL CHICKEN ROLLS

Crispy rolls. Allow a little extra time for these.

Ground raw chicken	½ lb.	225 g
Sliced green onion	⅓ cup	75 mL
Finely chopped celery	⅓ cup	75 mL
Grated carrot	¼ cup	60 mL
Chopped fresh mushrooms	½ cup	125 mL
Garlic cloves, minced (or ½ tsp., 2 mL, garlic powder)	2	2
Fresh bean sprouts	2 cups	500 mL
Oyster sauce	¼ cup	60 mL
Sherry (or alcohol-free sherry)	1 tbsp.	15 mL
Granulated sugar	1 tsp.	5 mL
Cornstarch	2 tsp.	10 mL
Toasted sesame seeds	1 tbsp.	15 mL
Frozen phyllo pastry sheets (about 1 lb., 454 g), thawed according to package directions	16	16
Hard margarine (or butter), melted	6 tbsp.	100 mL
Toasted sesame seeds	1 tbsp.	15 mL

Sauté first 6 ingredients in non-stick frying pan until chicken is golden and no pink remains.

Add bean sprouts. Sauté for 2 minutes.

Mix oyster sauce, sherry, sugar and cornstarch in small cup. Stir into vegetable mixture until mixture is boiling and thickened. Cool.

Add first amount of sesame seeds. Stir. If filling becomes watery while standing, drain liquid. Makes 3 cups (750 mL) filling.

Lay 1 pastry sheet on working surface. Cover remaining sheets with damp tea towel. Working quickly, brush sheet on working surface with melted margarine. Lay a second sheet over top. Brush with margarine. ❶ Cut into 6 squares. ❷ Place about 1 tbsp. (15 mL) filling on 1 corner. ❸ Fold corner over filling, tucking in sides. ❹ Roll to opposite corner, enclosing filling in finger-size roll. Repeat with remaining 14 sheets, using 2 each time. Brush each roll with remaining margarine.

Sprinkle rolls with second amount of sesame seeds. Arrange on ungreased baking sheet. Bake in 350°F (175°C) oven for about 20 minutes until golden. Makes 48.

1 roll: 50 Calories; 1.8 g Total Fat; 187 mg Sodium; 2 g Protein; 6 g Carbohydrate; trace Dietary Fiber

Pictured on page 125.

(continued on next page)

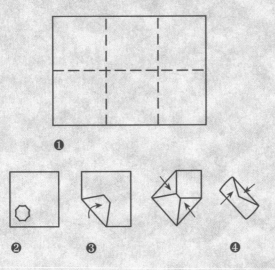

TORTILLA PINWHEELS

Nifty little rolls.

Creamed cottage cheese	2 cups	500 mL
Hard margarine (or butter)	1/4 cup	60 mL
Milk	2 tbsp.	30 mL
Lemon juice	1 tbsp.	15 mL
Chopped green onion	1/2 cup	125 mL
Canned diced green chilies, drained	4 oz.	114 mL
Grated medium Cheddar cheese	1 cup	250 mL
Garlic salt	1/4 tsp.	1 mL
Flour tortillas (8 inch, 20 cm, size)	12	12

Place first 4 ingredients in blender. Process until smooth. Turn into medium bowl.

Add green onion, green chilies, cheese and garlic salt. Stir.

Spread 1/4 cup (60 mL) cheese mixture on each tortilla. Roll up like jelly roll. Wrap in plastic wrap, sealing ends. Chill for at least 2 hours. Cut each roll into 10 slices, for a total of 120.

1 slice: 22 Calories; 0.8 g Total Fat; 50 mg Sodium; 1 g Protein; 2 g Carbohydrate; trace Dietary Fiber

SALAMI ROLLS

Filled with a tasty, zippy spread.

Cream cheese, softened	4 oz.	125 g
Grated onion	1 tbsp.	15 mL
Prepared horseradish	2 tsp.	10 mL
Beef bouillon powder	¼ tsp.	1 mL
Apple juice (or milk)	2 tbsp.	30 mL
Chopped chives	1 tsp.	5 mL
Very thin dry salami (or summer sausage) slices (3½ inches, 9 cm, in diameter), about ¼ lb. (113 g)	18	18

Mash first 6 ingredients well in small bowl. Add a bit more apple juice if needed to make spreadable.

Spread about 2 tsp. (10 mL) cream cheese mixture on each salami slice. Roll up. Place in covered container. Chill for 1 hour. Cut each roll into 3 slices, for a total of 54.

1 slice: 17 Calories; 1.5 g Total Fat; 48 mg Sodium; 1 g Protein; trace Carbohydrate; trace Dietary Fiber

Pictured on front cover.

MINI EGG ROLLS

Definitely a good choice. The shape is familiar but the size is definitely appetizer finger food.

Cooking oil	2 tbsp.	30 mL
Cooked chicken, diced and lightly packed	⅓ cup	75 mL
Fresh bean sprouts	½ lb.	225 g
Slivered onion	¼ cup	60 mL
Slivered celery	¼ cup	60 mL
Shredded cabbage	¼ cup	60 mL
Water	1 tbsp.	15 mL
Salt	½ tsp.	2 mL
Square wonton wrappers	84	84
Cooking oil, for deep-frying		

(continued on next page)

Heat first amount of cooking oil in frying pan until hot. Add next 5 ingredients. Stir-fry for 2 to 3 minutes.

Add water and salt. Cover. Steam for 1 minute. Cool.

Place ½ tsp. (2 mL) cooled filling on each wrapper, diagonally off center closer to 1 corner. Fold point over filling. Moisten open edges with water. Fold side points in over filling. Roll to opposite corner. Seal well.

When almost ready to serve, deep-fry in hot 375°F (190°C) cooking oil until golden. Makes 84.

1 roll: 18 Calories; 1.2 g Total Fat; 29 mg Sodium; trace Protein; 1 g Carbohydrate; trace Dietary Fiber

CHILI ROLLS

Pretty and bright with red and green clearly visible in the creamy filling.

Light cream cheese, softened	8 oz.	250 g
Milk	1 tbsp.	15 mL
Canned diced green chilies, drained	4 oz.	114 mL
Chopped ripe olives	2 tbsp.	30 mL
Finely chopped pecans	2 tbsp.	30 mL
Chopped chives	2 tbsp.	30 mL
Chopped pimientos	2 oz.	57 mL
Seasoned salt	⅛ tsp.	0.5 mL
Flour tortillas (8 inch, 20 cm, size)	6	6

Mash cream cheese and milk together in small bowl to make spreading consistency.

Add next 6 ingredients. Mix well.

Divide among tortillas. Spread evenly to edge. Roll up like jelly roll. Wrap each roll in plastic wrap. Refrigerate for several hours. Trim ends. Cut each roll into 10 slices, for a total of 60.

1 slice: 22 Calories; 0.9 g Total Fat; 69 mg Sodium; 1 g Protein; 3 g Carbohydrate; trace Dietary Fiber

Pictured on page 35.

SUSHI

Easier to make every time you try. Really good when slices are sprinkled with wasabi mixture.

Short grain white rice	1¼ cups	300 mL
Water	2½ cups	625 mL
Rice (or white) vinegar	2 tbsp.	30 mL
Granulated sugar	4 tsp.	20 mL
Salt	1 tsp.	5 mL
Sherry (or rice wine, such as sake, or alcohol-free sherry)	2 tbsp.	30 mL
Nori (roasted seaweed) sheets (available in Oriental section of grocery store)	4	4
Wasabi paste (available in Oriental section of grocery store) or 2 tbsp. (30 mL) mayonnaise	2 tsp.	10 mL

FILLING (Choose 3 or 4 for each roll)
Roasted red pepper, peeled, seeded and cut into slivers
Carrot, cut into 3 inch (7.5 cm) slivers
Green onion, cut into 3 inch (7.5 cm) slivers
English cucumber (with peel), cut into 3 inch (7.5 cm) slivers
Fresh asparagus spears, cooked and cooled
Avocado, peeled and cut into thin slices (see Note)
Fresh spinach leaves, cut into shreds
Large fried egg, with pierced yolk, cut into shreds
Canned (or imitation) crabmeat, cut into shreds

Combine first 5 ingredients in medium saucepan. Cover. Simmer for 25 to 30 minutes until rice is tender and most liquid is absorbed.

Stir in sherry. Cool.

❶ Lay 1 sheet of nori on small bamboo mat or heavy cloth napkin to assist in rolling. Spread 1 cup (250 mL) rice, using a wet fork, over nori to edge on 3 sides, leaving about 2 inches (5 cm) on long side, farthest away from you.

Spread with ¼ of wasabi paste.

(continued on next page)

Filling: ❷ Lay your choice of 3 or 4 of fillings in strip 1 inch (2.5 cm) wide, about 1 inch (2.5 cm) up from edge closest to you. Moisten nori with water on plain edge. ❸ Starting at long edge nearest you, roll up tightly using mat or cloth napkin to assist, rolling back and forth to pack tightly. Repeat with remaining 3 sheets of nori. Wrap in plastic wrap. Chill. Trim ends with wet sharp knife. Cut each roll into 5 slices, for a total of 20.

1 slice (without sauce): 93 Calories; 3.1 g Total Fat; 211 mg Sodium; 3 g Protein; 13 g Carbohydrate; 1 g Dietary Fiber

Pictured on front cover.

Note: Dip avocado slices into lemon juice to prevent darkening.

Variation: If you prefer not to use wasabi paste in the sushi, make a dipping sauce of ½ tsp. (2 mL) wasabi paste (or more, to taste) and ½ cup (125 mL) soy sauce.

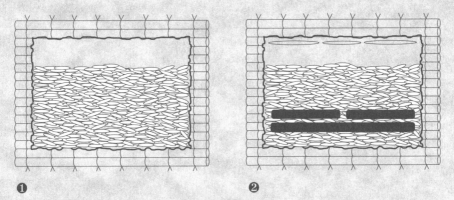

❶   ❷

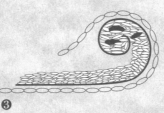

❸

Pancakes with dents are called waffles.

DOLMADES

Pronounced dohl-MAH-dehs. A Greek favorite. These are served at room temperature or hot as a sit-down starter.

Finely chopped onion	1½ cups	375 mL
Olive oil	2 tbsp.	30 mL
Chopped pine nuts (or pecans)	½ cup	125 mL
Basmati (or long grain white) rice	1 cup	250 mL
Water	2 cups	500 mL
Raisins	⅔ cup	150 mL
Parsley flakes (or ¼ cup, 60 mL, chopped fresh)	1 tbsp.	15 mL
Salt	1 tsp.	5 mL
Pepper	⅛ tsp.	0.5 mL
Ground cinnamon	¼ tsp.	1 mL
Seeded and chopped tomato	1 cup	250 mL
Jar of grapevine leaves	17 oz.	473 mL
Lemon juice	1½ tbsp.	25 mL
Olive oil	2 tbsp.	30 mL
Water	1 cup	250 mL

Sauté onion in first amount of olive oil in frying pan until soft.

Add pine nuts. Cook for 5 minutes until browned.

Add rice, first amount of water, raisins and parsley. Stir. Bring to a gentle boil. Cover. Simmer for 15 to 20 minutes until rice is cooked and liquid is absorbed.

Stir in salt, pepper, cinnamon, and tomato. Cool enough to handle.

Rinse vine leaves under warm water. Drain. Blot dry with tea towel or paper towels. Place about 2½ tbsp. (37 mL) rice mixture on each vine leaf. Roll stem end over rice, tucking in sides as you roll to completely enclose rice. Cover bottom and sides of greased 2 quart (2 L) casserole with vine leaves. Arrange, seam side down, close together over leaves.

Sprinkle with lemon juice and second amount of olive oil. Cover surface with any remaining grape leaves. Add second amount of water. Cover. Bake in 350°F (175°C) oven for about 1 hour. Cool. Serve with a sprinkle of lemon juice. Makes 32.

1 dolmade: 66 Calories; 3.2 g Total Fat; 86 mg Sodium; 1 g Protein; 9 g Carbohydrate; 1 g Dietary Fiber

Pictured on page 53.

Good starter for a Mexican meal. Serve with sour cream. Olé.

Sausage meat	**1 lb.**	**454 g**
Chopped onion	**½ cup**	**125 mL**
Salt	**¾ tsp.**	**4 mL**
Pepper	**¼ tsp.**	**1 mL**
Commercial pizza sauce	**¾ cup**	**175 mL**
Dried whole oregano	**¼ tsp.**	**1 mL**
Flour tortillas (8 inch, 20 cm, size)	**6**	**6**
Grated part-skim mozzarella cheese	**1½ cups**	**375 mL**

Scramble-fry sausage meat and onion in frying pan until no pink remains in meat and onion is soft. Drain. Mix in salt and pepper. Cool.

Stir pizza sauce, oregano and meat mixture in small bowl. Makes 2 cups (500 mL) filling.

Spread ⅓ cup (75 mL) filling over each tortilla. Sprinkle with ¼ cup (60 mL) cheese. Roll up as tightly as possible, like jelly roll. Wrap in plastic wrap. Chill until shortly before serving. Place on greased baking sheet. Bake in 400°F (205°C) oven for 7 to 8 minutes until cheese is melted. Trim ends. ❶ Cut each roll into 4 slices, for a total of 24.

1 slice: 87 Calories; 4.6 g Total Fat; 270 mg Sodium; 4 g Protein; 7 g Carbohydrate; trace Dietary Fiber

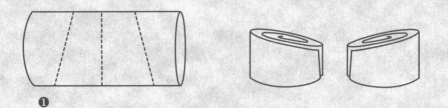

❶

ASPARAGUS ROLLS

Golden brown with asparagus, bacon and cheese showing.

White (or whole wheat) sandwich bread slices, crusts removed	16-18	16-18
Process cheese spread	¾ cup	175 mL
Bacon slices, cooked crisp and processed in blender or meat grinder	12	12
Canned (or fresh, cooked) asparagus spears	16-18	16-18
Hard margarine (or butter), melted	3 tbsp.	50 mL
Grated Parmesan cheese	1½ tbsp.	25 mL

Roll bread slices fairly flat with rolling pin.

Spread each slice with about 2 tsp. (10 mL) cheese spread. Sprinkle each with ¾ tsp. (4 mL) ground bacon. Lay asparagus spear on end of each slice, cutting off overhanging stem. Roll up snugly, like jelly roll. Secure with wooden pick if needed.

Brush each roll with melted margarine. Sprinkle with Parmesan cheese. Arrange on ungreased baking sheet. Bake in 400°F (205°C) oven for 7 to 8 minutes until golden or broil 6 inches (15 cm) from heat for 2 to 3 minutes until browned. Cut each roll in half, for a total of 32 to 36. Do not freeze.

*1 **half:** 78 Calories; 4.1 g Total Fat; 251 mg Sodium; 3 g Protein; 7 g Carbohydrate; trace Dietary Fiber*

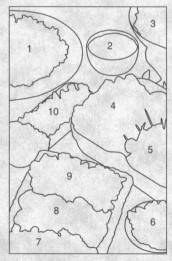

Props Courtesy Of: Eaton's   Handworks Gallery
Scona Clayworks   Stokes
The Basket House   The Bay

A bit more time is needed to make these. They do disappear quickly.
Serve with Simple Sweet And Sour Sauce, page 41.

Ground raw chicken	½ lb.	225 g
Chopped fresh mushrooms	1½ cups	375 mL
Sesame (or cooking) oil	2 tsp.	10 mL
Salt	1 tsp.	5 mL
Granulated sugar	1 tsp.	5 mL
Ground ginger	1 tsp.	5 mL
Garlic powder	¼ tsp.	1 mL
Green onions, thinly sliced	4	4
Grated carrot	½ cup	125 mL
Chopped fresh bean sprouts	3 cups	750 mL
Oyster sauce	2 tbsp.	30 mL
Sherry (or alcohol-free sherry)	1 tbsp.	15 mL
Egg roll wrappers (about 25)	1 lb.	454 g

Cooking oil, for deep-frying

Scramble-fry ground chicken and mushrooms in sesame oil in frying pan until no pink remains in chicken and liquid is evaporated.

Sprinkle with salt, sugar, ginger and garlic. Stir. Add green onion, carrot and bean sprouts. Stir-fry over medium-high for about 5 minutes until liquid is evaporated.

Stir in oyster sauce and sherry. Stir-fry for 1 minute.

Place about 2 tbsp. (30 mL) filling on each wrapper, diagonally off center closer to 1 corner. Fold point over filling. Moisten open edges with water. Fold side points in over filling. Roll to opposite corner. Seal well.

Deep-fry in hot 375°F (190°C) cooking oil for about 5 minutes until golden. Drain on paper towel. Makes 25.

1 roll: 85 Calories; 1.9 g Total Fat; 336 mg Sodium; 4 g Protein; 12 g Carbohydrate; 1 g Dietary Fiber

Pictured on page 125

LETTUCE WRAPS

Wrap filling in crisp lettuce leaves or leaf lettuce. An unusual treat to be sure.

Cooking oil	1 tsp.	5 mL
Boneless, skinless chicken breast half (about 4 oz., 113 g), cut into ½ inch (12 mm) dice	1	1
Grated carrot	¼ cup	60 mL
Sliced onion, in 1 inch (2.5 cm) long slivers	¼ cup	60 mL
Green pepper slivers	1 tbsp.	15 mL
Red pepper slivers	1 tbsp.	15 mL
Orange pepper slivers	1 tbsp.	15 mL
Water	¼ cup	60 mL
Package chicken-flavored Oriental soup noodles, broken into 6 pieces, seasoning packet reserved	1 × 3½ oz.	1 × 100 g
Reserved seasoning packet	½	½
Hoisin sauce	1 tbsp.	15 mL
Liquid honey	1 tsp.	5 mL
Pepper	⅛ tsp.	0.5 mL
Chili powder	¹⁄₁₆ tsp.	0.5 mL
Garlic powder	¹⁄₁₆ tsp.	0.5 mL
Hot pepper sauce	¼ tsp.	1 mL
Unsalted peanuts	¼ cup	60 mL
Lettuce leaves, from leaf or butter lettuce	8	8

Heat cooking oil in frying pan. Add chicken. Scramble-fry until no pink remains in meat.

Add carrot, onion and pepper slivers. Stir-fry until vegetables are tender crisp.

Add water. Stir in noodles. Cover. Simmer for about 2 minutes to soften.

Add next 8 ingredients. Stir well to heat through. Turn into small bowl.

(continued on next page)

Serve on platter with lettuce leaves. Have each person spoon about ⅛ of mixture onto leaf, roll it and eat. Makes about 8.

1 wrap: 103 Calories; 3.4 g Total Fat; 140 mg Sodium; 6 g Protein; 12 g Carbohydrate; 1 g Dietary Fiber

Pictured on page 125.

DEEP-FRIED PASTA

Tasty and crunchy. Be sure to try the variations to find your favorite.

Interesting-shaped pasta (such as rotini or tortiglioni), about	**4 cups**	**1 L**
Cooking oil, for deep-frying		
Grated Parmesan cheese	**¼ cup**	**60 mL**
Seasoned salt	**1 tsp.**	**5 mL**

Cook pasta according to package directions. Drain. Blot dry with paper towel.

Deep-fry in hot 375°F (190°C) cooking oil for 10 to 12 minutes until light golden brown, being careful not to overcook. With slotted spoon, transfer to paper towel-lined pan to drain. Do not cool. Place in large bowl.

While still hot, sprinkle with cheese and seasoned salt. Toss to coat. Makes about 4 cups (1 L).

¼ cup (60 mL): 84 Calories; 3.6 g Total Fat; 152 mg Sodium; 3 g Protein; 10 g Carbohydrate; 1 g Dietary Fiber

Variation #1: Add ½ tsp. (2 mL) cayenne pepper to seasoned salt.

Pictured on page 107.

Variation #2: Omit Parmesan cheese. Add same amount dry Cheddar cheese product.

Pictured on page 107.

TEXAS WHEELIES: Use wagon wheel pasta. Omit Parmesan cheese. Add same amount dry Cheddar cheese product and ½ tsp. (2 mL) chili powder to seasoned salt.

VEGGIE CHIPS

Make your own batch of colorful deep-fried vegetable chips.

Sweet potato, long and narrow, peeled	1	1
Medium parsnip, peeled	1	1
Medium carrot, peeled	1	1
Medium russet (or baking) potato, peeled	1	1
Ice water		
Cooking oil, for deep-frying		
Salt, sprinkle		

Using vegetable peeler, peel long thin strips from vegetables. Soak strips in large bowl in ice water for 30 minutes. Blot with paper towel or dry tea towel.

Deep-fry in batches in hot 375°F (190°C) cooking oil for about 2 minutes. Remove with slotted spoon to paper towels to drain. They should just be starting to brown. Cool. If not crisp, repeat deep-frying process, stirring continually for about 1 minute until crisp and beginning to brown. Remove with slotted spoon to paper towels to drain.

Sprinkle with salt. Cool thoroughly. Pile into large bowl. Makes about 10 cups (2.5 L).

¹/₄ cup (60 mL): 28 Calories; 2.3 g Total Fat; 2 mg Sodium; trace Protein; 2 g Carbohydrate; trace Dietary Fiber

Pictured on page 89.

CHEDDAR POPCORN

A great munchie.

Popped corn (pop about 1 cup, 250 mL)	6 qts.	6 L
Hard margarine (or butter)	¹/₂ cup	125 mL
Grated cheese product (powdered yellow Cheddar)	¹/₂ cup	125 mL
Garlic salt	¹/₄ tsp.	1 mL
Onion salt	¹/₄ tsp.	1 mL

(continued on next page)

Put popcorn into extra large container such as large roaster or preserving kettle.

Melt margarine in small saucepan.

Measure cheese into small bowl. Add garlic salt and onion salt. Stir well. Drizzle margarine over popcorn. Sprinkle with cheese mixture. Toss well. Makes 24 cups (6 L).

1 cup (250 mL): 79 Calories; 5 g Total Fat; 88 mg Sodium; 2 g Protein; 7 g Carbohydrate; 1 g Dietary Fiber

Pictured on page 107.

TORTILLA CHIPS

When making your own you have a choice of deep-frying or baking.

Corn tortillas (6 inch, 15 cm, size)	**12**	**12**
Cooking oil, for deep-frying		

Salt (or seasoned salt), sprinkle

Cut each tortilla into 8 wedges. Deep-fry several at a time in hot 375°F (190°C) cooking oil, turning occasionally, until crisp. Transfer to paper towels to drain.

Sprinkle with salt. Makes 96.

4 chips: 72 Calories; 3.8 g Total Fat; 35 mg Sodium; 1 g Protein; 9 g Carbohydrate; 1 g Dietary Fiber

Pictured on page 35.

OVEN TORTILLA CHIPS: Arrange wedges in single layer on ungreased baking sheets. Brush lightly with water. Sprinkle with salt. Bake in 400°F (205°C) oven for about 8 minutes. Turn wedges over. Bake for about 3 minutes.

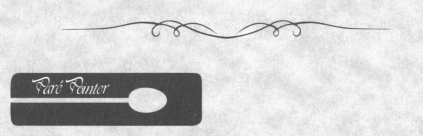

Paré Pointer

They bought a lot of ducks to try to improve their income. But they aren't picking up, they're picking down.

GOOD OL' NUTS 'N' BOLTS

Wonderful variety of shapes. A nice toasted flavor with a subtle taste of spices.

Small wheat squares cereal (such as Shreddies)	2 cups	500 mL
"O"-shaped toasted oat cereal (such as Cheerios)	1 cup	250 mL
Thin pretzels, broken in half	1 cup	250 mL
Rice and corn squares cereal (such as Crispix)	2 cups	500 mL
Mini snack crackers (such as Ritz Bits)	2 cups	500 mL
Mixed nuts	2 cups	500 mL
Hard margarine (or butter)	¼ cup	60 mL
Cooking oil	¼ cup	60 mL
Worcestershire sauce	2 tbsp.	30 mL
Garlic salt	1 tsp.	5 mL
Celery salt	1 tsp.	5 mL
Onion salt	1 tsp.	5 mL
Seasoned salt	1 tsp.	5 mL

Combine first 6 ingredients in large roaster. Stir.

Heat remaining 7 ingredients in small saucepan, stirring occasionally, until margarine is melted. Drizzle over dry mixture. Toss together well. Bake, uncovered, in 250°F (120°C) oven for 1 hour, stirring every 20 minutes. Cool. Store in airtight containers. Makes generous 2 quarts (2 L).

¼ cup (60 mL): 129 Calories; 8.8 g Total Fat; 314 mg Sodium; 3 g Protein; 11 g Carbohydrate; 1 g Dietary Fiber

CANDY KISS POPCORN

Good to munch on anytime.

Popped corn (pop about 1 cup, 250 mL)	6 qts.	6 L
Peanuts (optional)	1 cup	250 mL
Granulated sugar	2 cups	500 mL
Water	½ cup	125 mL
Fancy molasses	½ cup	125 mL
Salt	½ tsp.	2 mL
Baking soda	1 tsp.	5 mL

(continued on next page)

Combine popcorn and peanuts in extra large container such as large roaster or preserving kettle.

Heat sugar, water, molasses and salt in heavy medium saucepan. Stir until sugar is dissolved. Boil until soft ball stage on candy thermometer and a teaspoonful forms soft ball in cold water. Remove from heat.

Sift in baking soda. Pour while foaming over popcorn mixture. Stir well until evenly coated. Turn out onto large greased baking sheets. Bake in 350°F (175°C) oven for 10 minutes to dry. Stir and break up large pieces while it cools. Makes 16 cups (4 L).

1 cup (250 mL): 192 Calories; 0.8 g Total Fat; 173 mg Sodium; 2 g Protein; 46 g Carbohydrate; 1 g Dietary Fiber

TORTILLA CRISPS

Quick to make and very tasty. Serve with Mexican-type dips or enjoy them as they are.

Hard margarine (or butter), softened	¾ cup	175 mL
Grated Parmesan cheese	½ cup	125 mL
Parsley flakes	2 tsp.	10 mL
Sesame seeds	¼ cup	60 mL
Dried whole oregano	½ tsp.	2 mL
Onion powder	¼ tsp.	1 mL
Garlic powder	¼ tsp.	1 mL
Flour tortillas (6 inch, 15 cm, size)	12	12

Combine first 7 ingredients in small bowl. Mix well.

Spread each tortilla with thick layer of cheese mixture. It will seem like too much but once cooked they will be just right. Cut each tortilla into 8 wedges. Arrange in single layer on ungreased baking sheets. Bake in 350°F (175°C) oven for 12 to 15 minutes until crisp and browned. Makes 96.

4 chips: 129 Calories; 7.8 g Total Fat; 182 mg Sodium; 3 g Protein; 12 g Carbohydrate; trace Dietary Fiber

Pictured on page 35.

SPICED NUTS

Make lots of these days before you need them.

Egg white (large), room temperature	1	1
Water	2 tsp.	10 mL
Mixed nuts (or salted peanuts)	2 cups	500 mL
Granulated sugar	½ cup	125 mL
Ground cinnamon	1 tsp.	5 mL
Ground nutmeg	½ tsp.	2 mL
Ground ginger	¼ tsp.	1 mL
Salt	⅛ tsp.	0.5 mL

Beat egg white and water in medium bowl until smooth.

Stir in nuts.

Mix remaining 5 ingredients in small bowl. Add to nuts. Stir to coat. Spread on greased baking sheet. Bake in 250°F (120°C) oven for 1 hour, stirring every 15 minutes. Store in covered container or freeze. Makes 2 cups (500 mL).

¼ cup (60 mL): 269 Calories; 18.7 g Total Fat; 55 mg Sodium; 7 g Protein; 23 g Carbohydrate; 2 g Dietary Fiber

ORANGE PECANS

Delicious candied nuts. Nice orange aftertaste.

Granulated sugar	½ cup	125 mL
Pecan halves	2 cups	500 mL
Grated orange peel	1 tbsp.	15 mL
Prepared orange juice	¼ cup	60 mL

Combine all 4 ingredients in medium saucepan. Heat and stir until boiling. Boil, stirring constantly, until all liquid is absorbed. Turn out onto ungreased baking sheet. Separate pecans. Cool. Makes about 2¼ cups (560 mL).

¼ cup (60 mL): 221 Calories; 17.4 g Total Fat; trace Sodium; 2 g Protein; 17 g Carbohydrate; 2 g Dietary Fiber

Pictured on page 107.

PARTY CRACKERS

Good and crisp. Serve with a dip or spread.

Rye flour	1 cup	250 mL
All-purpose flour	1/2 cup	125 mL
Whole wheat flour	1/2 cup	125 mL
Salt	1/2 tsp.	2 mL
Baking soda	1/4 tsp.	1 mL
Celery salt	1/8 tsp.	0.5 mL
Water, approximately	1/2 cup	125 mL
Cooking oil	1/4 cup	60 mL

Measure all 3 flours, salt, baking soda and celery salt into medium bowl. Stir.

Add water and cooking oil. Mix into a ball, adding a touch more water if needed. Turn out onto lightly floured surface. Knead 20 times until smooth. Roll out 1/8 inch (3 mm) thick. Cut into 2 inch (5 cm) squares. Arrange on greased baking sheet in 275°F (140°C) oven for 30 to 40 minutes until browned. Makes about 50.

5 crackers: *136 Calories; 6.1 g Total Fat; 187 mg Sodium; 2 g Protein; 18 g Carbohydrate; 3 g Dietary Fiber*

Pictured on page 53.

ROASTED NUT SNACK

Dark in color. An intense flavor that keep you munching.

Soy sauce	1/2 cup	125 mL
Granulated sugar	1 tsp.	5 mL
Ground ginger	1/4 tsp.	1 mL
Garlic powder	1/4 tsp.	1 mL
Pecan halves (or peanuts)	3 cups	750 mL

Stir soy sauce, sugar, ginger and garlic in small bowl.

Add pecans. Stir well. Place pecans in greased 9 x 13 inch (22 x 33 cm) pan. Bake in 200°F (95°C) oven, stirring often, for about 1 hour until dried. Makes 3 cups (750 mL).

1/4 cup (60 mL): *203 Calories; 19.6 g Total Fat; 726 mg Sodium; 3 g Protein; 7 g Carbohydrate; 2 g Dietary Fiber*

SEASONED CRACKERS

Lots of garlic flavor on these.

Water	6 tbsp.	100 mL
Cornstarch	1 tsp.	5 mL
Envelope ranch-style salad dressing mix	1 × 1 oz.	1 × 28 g
Dill weed	1 tsp.	5 mL
Garlic powder	1/2 tsp.	2 mL
Garlic salt	1/2 tsp.	2 mL
Cooking oil	2 tbsp.	30 mL
Oyster (or other small snack) crackers	5 cups	1.25 L

Stir water and cornstarch together in small saucepan. Heat and stir until boiling and thickened. Remove from heat.

Whisk in next 5 ingredients.

Measure oyster crackers into large bowl. Add dill mixture. Toss and stir well. Spread on large ungreased baking sheet. Bake in 350°F (175°C) oven for 30 minutes, stirring several times. Makes 5 cups (1.25 L).

1/2 cup (125 mL): 154 Calories; 7.5 g Total Fat; 557 mg Sodium; 2 g Protein; 20 g Carbohydrate; trace Dietary Fiber

BAKED MIXED NUTS

Good munchies.

Cooking oil	1 tbsp.	15 mL
Chili powder	2 tsp.	10 mL
Garlic powder	1/2 tsp.	2 mL
Onion powder	1/2 tsp.	2 mL
Hot pepper sauce	1/2 tsp.	2 mL
Worcestershire sauce	1/2 tsp.	2 mL
Unsalted mixed nuts	2 cups	500 mL

Measure first 6 ingredients into medium bowl. Mix well.

Add nuts. Stir well to coat all nuts. Spread on ungreased baking sheet. Bake in 350°F (175°C) oven for 12 to 15 minutes until browned. Makes 2 cups (500 mL).

1/4 cup (60 mL): 234 Calories; 20.5 g Total Fat; 16 mg Sodium; 6 g Protein; 10 g Carbohydrate; 2 g Dietary Fiber

ROASTED GARLIC

Makes a nice soft spread. Serve with baguette slices or crackers. Or use as a condiment with hamburgers or steak. Roast several at a time if desired.

Whole garlic bulb	1	1
Olive oil	2 tbsp.	30 mL

Turn garlic bulb on its side. Cut top just so it cuts barely through tops of garlic cloves. Set bulb, cut side up, in garlic baker or small ungreased casserole.

Drizzle olive oil over center of bulb. Cover. Bake in 350°F (175°C) oven for about 40 minutes until it looks caramelized. Squeeze softened garlic out of top of bulb. Discard skin. Combine softened garlic and olive oil in bottom of casserole. Makes 2 tbsp. (30 mL).

1 tsp. (5 mL): 52 Calories; 4.6 g Total Fat; 1 mg Sodium; trace Protein; 2 g Carbohydrate; trace Dietary Fiber

SALMON BALL

Wonderful flavor and crunch as well. Make the variation to fit a cracker.

Canned red salmon, drained, skin and round bones removed, flaked	7½ oz.	213 g
Cream cheese, softened	8 oz.	250 g
Lemon juice	1 tbsp.	15 mL
Prepared horseradish	1 tbsp.	15 mL
Salt	¼ tsp.	1 mL
Finely chopped walnuts (or pecans), toasted	½ cup	125 mL

Mix first 5 ingredients well in medium bowl. Chill for at least 3 hours until mixture can be shaped. Shape into ball.

Roll ball in walnuts to coat. Chill in covered container. Makes 1¾ cups (425 mL).

1 tbsp. (15 mL): 54 Calories; 4.9 g Total Fat; 81 mg Sodium; 2 g Protein; 1 g Carbohydrate; trace Dietary Fiber

Variation: Shape into small balls, using 1½ tsp. (7 mL) mixture, each. Roll in finely chopped walnuts or pecans. Makes 56.

TUNA PÂTÉ

Bring to room temperature before serving. Just the right spreading consistency. Serve with assorted crackers or Toast Cups, page 14.

Cream cheese, softened	8 oz.	250 g
Chili sauce	2 tbsp.	30 mL
Chopped chives	2 tsp.	10 mL
Parsley flakes	2 tsp.	10 mL
Onion powder	¹/₂ tsp.	2 mL
Hot pepper sauce	1 tsp.	5 mL
Chopped green onion	2 tbsp.	30 mL
Canned tuna, drained and flaked	2 × 6¹/₂ oz.	2 × 184 g
Chopped fresh dill (or ¹/₂ tsp., 2 mL, dill weed)	2 tsp.	10 mL
CREAM CHEESE FROSTING		
Cream cheese, softened	4 oz.	125 g
Skim evaporated milk (or light cream)	1 tbsp.	15 mL

Mix all 9 ingredients well in large bowl. Shape by hand into round or oblong mound on serving dish. Chill before frosting.

Cream Cheese Frosting: Beat cream cheese and evaporated milk together well. Frost top and sides of pâté mound. Chill. Makes 2¹/₂ cups (625 mL).

1 tbsp. (15 mL): 42 Calories; 3.3 g Total Fat; 65 mg Sodium; 3 g Protein; 1 g Carbohydrate; trace Dietary Fiber

CRAB DELUXE

Have this in the refrigerator for a ready-to-serve tasty treat. Serve with crackers.

Cream cheese, softened	12 oz.	340 g
Salad dressing (or mayonnaise)	¹/₄ cup	60 mL
Worcestershire sauce	2 tbsp.	30 mL
White vinegar	1 tsp.	5 mL
Minced mild onion	¹/₄ cup	60 mL
Chili sauce	¹/₂ cup	125 mL
Canned crabmeat, drained and cartilage removed	2 × 4¹/₄ oz.	2 × 120 g
Chopped green onion (or chives)	2 tbsp.	30 mL

(continued on next page)

Mix first 5 ingredients in medium bowl until smooth. Spread over ungreased 12 inch (30 cm) serving plate or pizza pan.

Spread chili sauce over top, keeping in about ½ inch (12 mm) from edge. Sprinkle crabmeat over chili sauce. Sprinkle with green onion. Cover. Chill for several hours so flavors will have a chance to blend. Makes about 3½ cups (875 mL).

1 tbsp. (15 mL): 30 Calories; 2.6 g Total Fat; 77 mg Sodium; 1 g Protein; 1 g Carbohydrate; trace Dietary Fiber

LOG O' CHEESE

A very different coating for this log. Sesame seeds add a great flavor.

Grated sharp Cheddar cheese, lightly packed	2 cups	500 mL
Salad dressing (or mayonnaise)	¼ cup	60 mL
Sweet pickle relish	2 tbsp.	30 mL
Seasoned salt	½ tsp.	2 mL
Onion powder	½ tsp.	2 mL
Minced green pepper	3 tbsp.	50 mL
Roasted red pepper, chopped (or chopped pimiento)	1 tbsp.	15 mL
Large hard-boiled egg, finely chopped	1	1
Saltine cracker crumbs	½ cup	125 mL
Sesame seeds	¼ cup	60 mL

Mix first 5 ingredients well in medium bowl.

Add next 4 ingredients. Mix well. Shape into roll, 1½ inches (3.8 cm) in diameter and about 9 inches (22 cm) long. Wrap in waxed paper. Chill for at least 1 hour to firm.

Spread sesame seeds over bottom of ungreased 9 x 13 inch (22 x 33 cm) pan. Toast in 350°F (175°C) oven for 5 to 10 minutes until lightly toasted. Set cheese log at end. Roll over warm seeds to coat. Wrap in waxed paper. Chill until ready to serve. Makes 1 log, about 2 cups (500 mL). Cuts into 36 slices.

1 slice: 50 Calories; 3.9 g Total Fat; 90 mg Sodium; 2 g Protein; 2 g Carbohydrate; trace Dietary Fiber

SHRIMP MOUSSE

A real party attraction. Surround with a variety of crackers or cocktail-size dark bread squares.

Envelopes unflavored gelatin	2 x ¼ oz.	2 x 7 g
Water	½ cup	125 mL
Cream cheese, softened	8 oz.	250 g
Condensed tomato soup	10 oz.	284 mL
Salad dressing (or mayonnaise)	½ cup	125 mL
Lemon juice	2 tbsp.	30 mL
Salt	½ tsp.	2 mL
Onion powder	½ tsp.	2 mL
Worcestershire sauce	¼ tsp.	1 mL
Finely chopped celery	1 cup	250 mL
Finely chopped green pepper	⅓ cup	75 mL
Canned small (or broken) shrimp, drained, rinsed and chopped	2 x 4 oz.	2 x 113 g

Sprinkle gelatin over water in small saucepan. Let stand for 1 minute. Heat and stir until gelatin is dissolved. Remove from heat.

Beat cream cheese and tomato soup in small bowl until smooth. Beat in salad dressing, lemon juice, salt, onion powder and Worcestershire sauce. Add gelatin mixture. Stir well.

Fold in remaining 3 ingredients. Turn into 6 cup (1.5 L) mold. Chill. Makes 5½ cups (1.4 L).

1 tbsp. (15 mL): *42 Calories; 3.2 g Total Fat; 117 mg Sodium; 2 g Protein; 2 g Carbohydrate; trace Dietary Fiber*

APRICOT CHEESE SPREAD

One of the quickest, easiest and best. Serve with Party Crackers, page 117. Needs a cocktail spreader.

Cream cheese	8 oz.	250 g
Apricot jam	⅓ cup	75 mL
Dry mustard	1½ tsp.	7 mL
Apple cider vinegar	½ tsp.	2 mL

(continued on next page)

Set cream cheese block on serving plate.

Mix jam, mustard and vinegar in small bowl. Makes ⅓ cup (75 mL). Spoon over cream cheese, allowing some to run down sides. Makes about 16 servings.

1 serving: 75 Calories; 5.6 g Total Fat; 47 mg Sodium; 1 g Protein; 5 g Carbohydrate; trace Dietary Fiber

Pictured on page 53.

SALMON MOUSSE

A star attraction that will disappear quickly. Serve with Toast Cups, page 14, or an assortment of crackers.

Envelope unflavored gelatin	**1 x ¼ oz.**	**1 x 7 g**
Water	**½ cup**	**125 mL**
Salad dressing (or mayonnaise)	**½ cup**	**125 mL**
Sour cream	**¼ cup**	**60 mL**
Lemon juice	**1 tbsp.**	**15 mL**
Dill weed	**2 tsp.**	**10 mL**
Onion powder	**1 tsp.**	**5 mL**
Paprika	**1 tsp.**	**5 mL**
Hot pepper sauce	**½ tsp.**	**2 mL**
Salt	**¼ tsp.**	**1 mL**
Canned red salmon, drained, skin and bones removed, flaked	**7½ oz.**	**213 g**
Envelope dessert topping, prepared according to package directions	**1**	**1**

Sprinkle gelatin over water in small saucepan. Let stand for 1 minute. Heat and stir until gelatin is dissolved. Remove from heat. Cool.

Add next 8 ingredients. Whisk until well mixed. Chill, stirring often, until mixture starts to thicken.

Fold in salmon.

Fold dessert topping into salmon mixture. Turn into 4 cup (1 L) mold. Chill. Makes 4 cups (1 L).

2 tbsp. (30 mL): 40 Calories; 3.2 g Total Fat; 73 mg Sodium; 1 g Protein; 1 g Carbohydrate; trace Dietary Fiber

Paré Pointer

We should be like pianos, either upright or grand.

BRUSCHETTA BRIE

Wonderful basil and garlic flavor that everyone enjoys. Needs a cocktail spreader.

Small tomato, seeded and finely chopped	1	1
Garlic clove, crushed	1	1
Olive oil	1 tsp.	5 mL
Dried sweet basil, crushed	1½ tsp.	7 mL
Salt	¼ tsp.	1 mL
Pepper, sprinkle		
Brie cheese round, with rind	4 oz.	125 g
Baguette slices, toasted or plain	12	12

Combine first 6 ingredients in small bowl. Stir. Let stand at room temperature for 1 hour.

Set cheese round in ungreased small shallow casserole. Using slotted spoon, and allowing most liquid to drain off, transfer tomato mixture over top of cheese. Discard remaining liquid. Bake, uncovered, in 375°F (190°C) oven for 8 to 10 minutes until cheese is soft inside rind. Transfer with pancake lifter to serving plate.

Surround with baguette slices. Makes 12 appetizer servings.

1 serving: *151 Calories; 4.1 g Total Fat; 343 mg Sodium; 6 g Protein; 22 g Carbohydrate; 1 g Dietary Fiber*

Pictured on page 53.

1 Lettuce Wraps, page 110
2. Beef Buns, page 28
3. Hot And Sour Soup, page 150
4. Oriental Chicken Rolls, page 98
5. Crab Rangoon, page 58
6. Spring Rolls, page 109
7. Simple Sweet And Sour Sauce, page 41
8. Sprout Salad, page 140
9. Salad Rolls, page 96

Props Courtesy Of: Eaton's
Kitchen Treasures
Scona Clayworks
The Bay

SAVORY CHEESECAKE

Serve a slightly larger wedge for a sit-down starter, or surround the smaller appetizer wedges with raw vegetables and taco chips on a platter.

CRUST

Hard margarine (or butter)	½ cup	125 mL
Soda cracker crumbs	1½ cups	375 mL
Grated Parmesan cheese	¼ cup	60 mL

FILLING

Cream cheese, softened	2 × 8 oz.	2 × 250 g
Grated Monterey Jack cheese	1 cup	250 mL
Grated sharp Cheddar cheese	1 cup	250 mL
Sour cream	1 cup	250 mL
Onion powder	½ tsp.	2 mL
Salt	¼ tsp.	1 mL
Pepper	⅛ tsp.	0.5 mL
Large eggs	3	3
Canned diced green chilies, drained	4 oz.	114 mL

TOPPING

Salsa	½ cup	125 mL

Crust: Melt margarine in medium saucepan. Add cracker crumbs and Parmesan cheese. Mix. Press in bottom of ungreased 9 inch (22 cm) springform pan. Bake in 350°F (175°C) oven for 10 minutes. Cool.

Filling: Combine first 7 ingredients in large bowl. Beat until smooth and creamy.

Slowly beat in 1 egg at a time, beating after each addition until just mixed. Add green chilies. Stir. Pour over crust. Bake for 50 minutes until center is barely firm. Remove from oven. Immediately run paring knife around top edge so cheesecake settles evenly. Cool. Refrigerate overnight.

Topping: Spread salsa over top of chilled cheesecake. Cuts into 20 wedges.

1 wedge: 246 Calories; 21.1 g Total Fat; 475 mg Sodium; 8 g Protein; 7 g Carbohydrate; trace Dietary Fiber

CHEESY CHILI BALL

Surround this full-flavored spread with your favorite crackers. Has a wee bit of a bite to it.

Cream cheese, softened	8 oz.	250 g
Process cheese loaf (such as Velveeta), room temperature	8 oz.	250 g
Grated medium Cheddar cheese	2 cups	500 mL
Chili powder	1½ tsp.	7 mL
Garlic powder	¼ tsp.	1 mL
Onion salt	¹⁄₁₆ tsp.	0.5 mL
Chopped pecans (or walnuts)	½ cup	125 mL

Mix first 6 ingredients well in medium bowl. Chill until firm enough to roll. Shape into ball.

Roll in pecans to coat. Cover with plastic wrap. Makes 3¼ cups (810 mL).

1 tbsp. (15 mL): 57 Calories; 5 g Total Fat; 117 mg Sodium; 2 g Protein; 1 g Carbohydrate; trace Dietary Fiber

BLUE CHEESE BALL

Just enough blue cheese to give a bit of a nip. Looks terrific either alone or surrounded with crackers.

Cream cheese, softened	8 oz.	250 g
Blue cheese, softened	4 oz.	125 g
Grated medium Cheddar cheese	2 cups	500 mL
Chopped pecans (or walnuts)	½ cup	125 mL
Parsley flakes	1 tbsp.	15 mL
Worcestershire sauce	1 tsp.	5 mL
Onion powder	½ tsp.	2 mL
Chopped pecans (or walnuts)	½ cup	125 mL

Combine first 7 ingredients in large bowl. Mix thoroughly. Shape into ball.

Put second amount of pecans onto working surface. Roll cheese ball in pecans to coat. Chill. Bring to room temperature just before serving for best flavor. Makes about 3 cups (750 mL).

1 tbsp. (15 mL): 62 Calories; 5.7 g Total Fat; 81 mg Sodium; 2 g Protein; 1 g Carbohydrate; trace Dietary Fiber

Individual salads on a lettuce bed look so neat.

Envelopes unflavored gelatin	**2 × ¼ oz.**	**2 × 7 g**
Water	**½ cup**	**125 mL**
Condensed tomato soup	**10 oz.**	**284 mL**
Cream cheese, cut up	**8 oz.**	**250 g**
Salad dressing (or mayonnaise)	**¾ cup**	**175 mL**
Sour cream	**¼ cup**	**60 mL**
Chopped pimiento-stuffed green olives	**¼ cup**	**60 mL**
Chopped celery	**½ cup**	**125 mL**
Onion powder	**¼ tsp.**	**1 mL**
Salt	**¼ tsp.**	**1 mL**
Granulated sugar	**1 tsp.**	**5 mL**
Shredded iceberg lettuce	**5 cups**	**1.25 L**
Thin slices peeled cucumber	**10**	**10**
Sour cream (or mayonnaise)	**2 tbsp.**	**30 mL**

Sprinkle gelatin over water in medium saucepan. Let stand for 1 minute. Heat and stir until gelatin is dissolved.

Add tomato soup. Mix well. Add cream cheese. Heat, stirring often, until cream cheese is melted. Use whisk or beater if necessary.

Whisk in salad dressing and first amount of sour cream. Add olives, celery, onion powder, salt and sugar. Stir well. Pour into 10 individual ⅓ cup (75 mL) salad molds. Chill for 20 minutes. Stir gently to distribute contents. Chill until firm.

Let stand at room temperature for 30 to 45 minutes for easy unmolding. Divide lettuce among 10 salad plates. Unmold aspic onto lettuce. Garnish each with cucumber slice. Place a dab of sour cream on top of each cucumber slice. Makes 10.

1 mold: 218 Calories; 19 g Total Fat; 554 mg Sodium; 4 g Protein; 9 g Carbohydrate; 1 g Dietary Fiber

What a noise. Ever since their cat ate their canary, it thinks it can sing.

SHRIMP PAPAYA SALAD

Just an incredible mixture of flavors. Very showy and so very good.

DILL SAUCE

Sour cream	¼ cup	60 mL
Salad dressing (or mayonnaise)	¼ cup	60 mL
Lemon juice	1 tsp.	5 mL
Dill weed	½ tsp.	2 mL
Granulated sugar	½ tsp.	2 mL
Lettuce cups	4	4
Papayas, peeled, seeded and diced	2	2
Cooked medium shrimp, peeled and deveined	1 cup	250 mL

Dill Sauce: Mix sour cream, salad dressing, lemon juice, dill weed and sugar in small bowl. This can be prepared ahead and chilled.

Lay 1 lettuce cup on each of 4 salad plates. Place ¼ of diced papaya on each lettuce leaf. Divide shrimp over papaya. Drizzle sauce over shrimp. Serves 4.

1 serving: 199 Calories; 10.4 g Total Fat; 185 mg Sodium; 9 g Protein; 19 g Carbohydrate; 3 g Dietary Fiber

Pictured on page 143.

PISTACHIO SALAD

A dramatic contrast is created with the dark green spinach leaves and the white cottage cheese. Very showy.

Canned fruit cocktail, drained	14 oz.	398 mL
Canned crushed pineapple, well drained	8 oz.	227 mL
Instant pistachio pudding powder, 4 serving size (add dry)	1	1
Creamed cottage cheese	2 cups	500 mL
Miniature marshmallows	1 cup	250 mL
Envelope dessert topping, prepared according to package directions	1	1
Shredded fresh spinach, packed	4 cups	1 L
Maraschino cherries, patted dry	8	8
Chopped pistachios (optional)	1 tbsp.	15 mL

(continued on next page)

Stir first 3 ingredients together well in large bowl.

Add cottage cheese and marshmallows. Stir. Fold in dessert topping.

Divide spinach among 8 salad plates. Use ice-cream scoop to place salad on spinach.

Top each with cherry. Add sprinkle of chopped pistachios. Serves 8.

1 serving: 196 Calories; 3.5 g Total Fat; 355 mg Sodium; 10 g Protein; 33 g Carbohydrate; 2 g Dietary Fiber

FRESH FRUIT SALAD

A festive-looking salad to pass around the table for a first course. Dressing is very tasty and clings well to the fruit.

APRICOT DRESSING		
Dried apricots	8	8
Boiling water, to cover		
Vanilla yogurt	¾ cup	175 mL
SALAD		
Whole fresh strawberries, halved	6	6
Kiwifruit, peeled and cut lengthwise into 6 wedges	4	4
Seedless red grapes, halved	18	18
Cantaloupe balls or pieces	24	24
Fresh blueberries	½ cup	125 mL
Thin red apple wedges, with peel, dipped into lemon juice	12	12

Apricot Dressing: Soak apricots in boiling water to cover for about 20 minutes. Drain. Transfer to blender.

Add yogurt. Process until smooth. Makes ¾ cup (175 mL) dressing.

Salad: Arrange assorted fruit on large plate, beginning with strawberries in center. Add rings of other fruit. Stand apple slices, skin side up, around top of fruit. Drizzle with dressing. Serves 6.

1 serving: 129 Calories; 1.3 g Total Fat; 35 mg Sodium; 4 g Protein; 29 g Carbohydrate; 4 g Dietary Fiber

BLUEBERRY STARTER

This is so good you could almost serve it for dessert.

Packages raspberry-flavored gelatin (jelly powder)	2 × 3 oz.	2 × 85 g
Boiling water	2 cups	500 mL
Reserved juice from blueberries and pineapple, plus water if needed to make	1 cup	250 mL
Canned blueberries, drained and juice reserved	14 oz.	398 mL
Canned crushed pineapple, drained and juice reserved	14 oz.	398 mL
CREAM CHEESE DRESSING		
Light cream cheese, softened	8 oz.	250 g
Granulated sugar	½ cup	125 mL
Light sour cream	1 cup	250 mL
Vanilla	1 tsp.	5 mL
Chopped pecans (or walnuts)	½ cup	125 mL
Lettuce cups	9	9

Combine gelatin and boiling water in medium bowl. Stir until gelatin is dissolved.

Add reserved juices. Stir. Chill, stirring and scraping down sides occasionally, until syrupy consistency.

Add blueberries and pineapple. Stir. Pour into ungreased 9 × 9 inch (22 × 22 cm) square pan. Chill until firm.

Cream Cheese Dressing: Beat cream cheese, sugar, sour cream and vanilla in medium bowl until smooth. Spread over jelled layer, or drizzle dressing over individual servings.

Sprinkle with pecans.

Set lettuce cup on each of 9 plates. Cut salad into 9 pieces. Set piece of salad in center of lettuce. Serves 9.

1 serving: 310 Calories; 10.9 g Total Fat; 306 mg Sodium; 6 g Protein; 50 g Carbohydrate; 2 g Dietary Fiber

Color, flavor, crunch and more flavor. This is the one.

NOODLES

Hard margarine (or butter)	1½ tbsp.	25 mL
Worcestershire sauce	1½ tsp.	7 mL
Seasoned salt	¼ tsp.	1 mL
Garlic salt	⅛ tsp.	0.5 mL
Onion powder	⅛ tsp.	0.5 mL
Curry powder	¼ tsp.	1 mL
Chow mein noodles	1 cup	250 mL

SALAD

Head of romaine lettuce, cut up	1	1
Green pepper slivers, 1-1½ inches (2.5-3.8 cm) long	⅔ cup	150 mL
Medium tomatoes, halved, seeded and cut into thin wedges	2	2

DRESSING

Salad dressing (or mayonnaise)	⅓ cup	75 mL
French dressing (red)	2 tbsp.	30 mL
Milk	2 tbsp.	30 mL
Granulated sugar	½ tsp.	2 mL

Noodles: Put first 6 ingredients into medium saucepan. Heat and stir until margarine is melted.

Add noodles. Stir well to coat. Spread on ungreased baking sheet. Bake in 250°F (120°C) oven for 15 minutes. Cool.

Salad: Toss all 3 ingredients together in large bowl.

Dressing: Measure all 4 ingredients into small bowl. Stir. Add to salad along with noodles. Toss. Makes 8 cups (2 L).

1 cup (250 mL): 141 Calories; 11.2 g Total Fat; 266 mg Sodium; 2 g Protein; 9 g Carbohydrate; 2 g Dietary Fiber

Paré Pointer

What colorful weather. The sun rose and the wind blew.

PINK SALAD MOLDS

Small salads with a creamy raspberry flavor. Lots of crunchy pecans.
Mousse consistency.

Package raspberry-flavored gelatin (jelly powder)	1 × 3 oz.	1 × 85 g
Boiling water	1 cup	250 mL
Cream cheese, softened	4 oz.	125 g
Canned crushed pineapple, well drained	8 oz.	227 mL
Envelope dessert topping, prepared according to package directions	1	1
Chopped pecans (or walnuts)	½ cup	125 mL
Lettuce cups	8	8

Stir gelatin and boiling water in medium bowl until gelatin is dissolved. Chill, stirring and scraping down sides occasionally, until syrupy consistency.

Mash cream cheese with fork in medium bowl until very soft. Add pineapple. Mix. Stir into thickened jelly.

Fold in dessert topping and pecans. This makes 4½ cups (1.1 L) jelly. Fill 8 individual molds, each holding about ½ cup (125 mL). Chill until set.

Set lettuce cup on each of 8 salad plates. Unmold salads onto lettuce cups. Serves 8.

1 serving: 191 Calories; 12.8 g Total Fat; 87 mg Sodium; 4 g Protein; 17 g Carbohydrate; 1 g Dietary Fiber

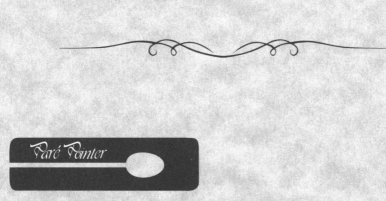

Paré Pointer

What else would invisible parents feed their baby but evaporated milk?

PICTURE BOOK SALAD

An artistic arrangement makes for a conversational presentation. These are almost too pretty to disturb.

POPPY SEED DRESSING

Granulated sugar	⅓ cup	75 mL
White vinegar	¼ cup	60 mL
Prepared mustard	1½ tsp.	7 mL
Prepared horseradish	¼ tsp.	1 mL
Salt	¼ tsp.	1 mL
Pepper, just a pinch		
Cooking oil	⅓ cup	75 mL
Poppy seeds	1½ tsp.	7 mL

SALAD

Chinese cabbage inner leaves	18	18
Paper-thin lengthwise slices of small English cucumber	18	18
Cantaloupe center ring slices, peeled	6	6
Red pepper ring slices	6	6
Strawberries (or cherry tomatoes), cut into fans, for garnish	18	18

Poppy Seed Dressing: Measure first 6 ingredients into blender. Process until smooth.

With blender running, add cooking oil in a slow steady stream until mixture has thickened.

Pour into container. Stir in poppy seeds. Chill until needed. Makes ⅔ cup (150 mL) dressing.

Salad: Arrange 3 cabbage leaves on each of 6 salad plates, placing leaves in spoke fashion out from center equal distance apart. Lay cucumber slice on each leaf, rounding ends that are visible. Set ring of cantaloupe in center. Place red pepper ring on top of cantaloupe.

Cut strawberries in slices from top almost to, but not through, bottom. Press gently to fan out. Set 1 in center of each red pepper ring. Place 1 between each pair of cabbage leaves. Drizzle about 2 tbsp. (30 mL) dressing over each salad. Serves 6.

1 serving: 190 Calories; 13.4 g Total Fat; 141 mg Sodium; 1 g Protein; 18 g Carbohydrate; 1 g Dietary Fiber

Pictured on page 143.

WHITE SALAD

A white salad nestled inside a green border.

Shredded dark green lettuce (such as romaine), packed	3 cups	750 mL
Sliced fresh white mushrooms	1½ cups	375 mL
Sliced center white ribs of celery	1½ cups	375 mL
Peeled and sliced radishes	½ cup	125 mL
Grated Monterey Jack cheese	¾ cup	175 mL
HONEY DRESSING		
Liquid honey	⅓ cup	75 mL
White vinegar	¼ cup	60 mL
Cooking oil	3 tbsp.	50 mL
Pepper, just a pinch		

Make outer ring of lettuce on each of 6 salad plates.

Divide mushrooms, celery and radish inside lettuce rings, leaving a border of green all around. Pile cheese in center.

Honey Dressing: Mix all 4 ingredients well in small bowl. Makes ⅔ cup (150 mL). Drizzle about 2 tbsp. (30 mL) over each salad. Serves 6.

1 serving: 194 Calories; 11.7 g Total Fat; 114 mg Sodium; 5 g Protein; 20 g Carbohydrate; 1 g Dietary Fiber

AVOCADO SALAD

Smooth creamy avocado takes center stage. Delicious.

Chili sauce	¼ cup	60 mL
Lemon juice	1 tbsp.	15 mL
Granulated sugar	4 tsp.	20 mL
Onion powder	¼ tsp.	1 mL
Worcestershire sauce	½ tsp.	2 mL
Salt	½ tsp.	2 mL
Celery salt	¼ tsp.	1 mL
Garlic powder	¼ tsp.	1 mL
Avocados, peeled and sliced	2	2
Salad greens, cut up	2 cups	500 mL

(continued on next page)

Stir first 8 ingredients together well in medium bowl.

Add avocado. Stir to coat well. Cover. Let stand in refrigerator for several hours or overnight, stirring gently once or twice.

Divide salad greens among each of 4 salad plates. Gently spoon avocado with dressing over greens. Serves 4.

1 serving: 205 Calories; 15.6 g Total Fat; 693 mg Sodium; 3 g Protein; 18 g Carbohydrate; 4 g Dietary Fiber

PARFAIT SALAD

Layers of crabmeat, lettuce and assorted vegetables. Topped with cheese, this is a novel presentation.

Salad dressing (or mayonnaise)	1/4 cup	60 mL
Sweet pickle relish	2 tsp.	10 mL
Finely chopped celery	2 tsp.	10 mL
Parsley flakes	1 tsp.	5 mL
Onion powder	1/8 tsp.	0.5 mL
Sour cream	3 tbsp.	50 mL
Salt	1/4 tsp.	1 mL
Milk	1 tbsp.	15 mL
Canned crabmeat, drained and cartilage removed	4 1/4 oz.	120 g
Large hard-boiled eggs, chopped	2	2
Chopped lettuce, packed	1 cup	250 mL
Green onions, thinly sliced	2	2
Cooked peas, cooled	1/2 cup	125 mL
Grated medium Cheddar cheese	1/4 cup	60 mL

Combine first 10 ingredients in medium bowl. Stir together.

Divide lettuce among 4 stemmed large wine or water goblets or other glassware. Even an old-fashioned glass will work.

Divide crab mixture over top, being careful not to smear edge of glass. Divide and layer green onion and peas over crabmeat.

Sprinkle 1 tbsp. (15 mL) cheese over each. Chill until serving time. Serves 4.

1 serving: 211 Calories; 15.1 g Total Fat; 565 mg Sodium; 11 g Protein; 8 g Carbohydrate; 1 g Dietary Fiber

SALAD HORNS

These little horns of plenty are impressive with a fruit and chicken filling and a curry dressing.

PASTRY HORNS

Frozen puff pastry (see Note), thawed according to package directions	½ × 14.1 oz.	½ × 397 g
Large egg, fork-beaten	1	1

SALAD

Cooked chicken, cut bite size	1 cup	250 mL
Diced celery	¼ cup	60 mL
Canned pineapple tidbits, drained and cut smaller (reserve remaining whole pieces for garnish)	¼ cup	60 mL
Seedless green grapes, quartered	½ cup	125 mL
Sliced almonds, toasted and chopped	¼ cup	60 mL
Salt, sprinkle		
Pepper, sprinkle		

CURRY DRESSING

Salad dressing (or mayonnaise)	¼ cup	60 mL
Lemon juice	¾ tsp.	4 mL
Soy sauce	¾ tsp.	4 mL
Curry powder, scant measure	½ tsp.	2 mL
Milk	1 tbsp.	15 mL

GARNISH

Seedless green grapes	12	12
Pimiento strips	12	12
Reserved pineapple tidbits, cut up		

Pastry Horns: Roll out pastry on lightly floured surface to 12 × 12 inch (30 × 30 cm) square. Cut into long strips about ¾ to 1 inch (2 to 2.5 cm) wide.

Brush 1 strip with egg. Turn strip over. ❶ Place pointed end of metal form at lower end of strip. ❷ Wind strip around form, overlapping edges slightly, working up towards open end. Place on greased baking sheet. Repeat with remaining strips. Bake in 425°F (220°C) oven for 15 to 20 minutes until golden brown. Let stand for 10 minutes. Gently push horns off metal forms.

(continued on next page)

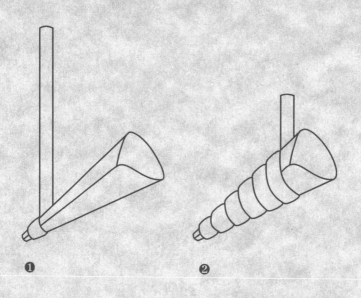

Salad: Combine all 7 ingredients in medium bowl. Toss. Chill until needed.

Curry Dressing: Stir all 5 ingredients together in small bowl. Chill until needed.

Set 1 pastry horn on each of 8 salad plates. Combine salad and dressing. Toss well. Gently spoon small amount into each horn. Spoon remaining salad spilling from horn.

Garnish: Place 2 grapes on 1 side of horn. Set 2 pimiento strips on salad. Divide remaining pineapple pieces alongside. Serves 8.

1 serving: 336 Calories; 22.2 g Total Fat; 392 mg Sodium; 10 g Protein; 24 g Carbohydrate; 1 g Dietary Fiber

Pictured on page 53.

Note: This much puff pastry will make 12 horns. Salad fills 8. Freeze remaining horns.

Paré Pointer

When a beautiful girl offers you a date and you would prefer a fig—you are beyond help.

SPROUT SALAD

Tangy dressing, crunchy sprouts, colorful red pepper slivers and more. As fresh as they come.

Chopped fresh bean sprouts	3 cups	750 mL
Green onion, chopped	1	1
Chopped fresh mushrooms	²/₃ cup	150 mL
Paper-thin slivers of red pepper, 1 inch (2.5 cm) long	¼ cup	60 mL
Apple cider vinegar	1 tbsp.	15 mL
Soy sauce	1 tbsp.	15 mL
Granulated sugar	½ tsp.	2 mL
Cooking oil	2 tsp.	10 mL
Lettuce cups (or shredded lettuce)	4	4

Combine bean sprouts, green onion, mushrooms and red pepper in medium bowl.

Mix vinegar, soy sauce, sugar and cooking oil in small cup. Stir well. Add to sprout mixture. Toss.

Set lettuce cup on each of 4 salad plates. Divide sprout mixture among them. Serves 4.

*1 **serving:** 57 Calories; 2.5 g Total Fat; 267 mg Sodium; 3 g Protein; 7 g Carbohydrate; 1 g Dietary Fiber*

Pictured on page 125.

CORN CHOWDER

Flavorful bacon is the star in this chowder. Great taste. Nice and chunky.

Bacon slices, diced	5	5
Chopped onion	½ cup	125 mL
Medium potatoes, peeled and diced	2	2
Water	1 cup	250 mL
Canned cream-style corn	2 × 14 oz.	2 × 398 mL
Salt	½ tsp.	2 mL
Pepper	¼ tsp.	1 mL
Parsley flakes	2 tsp.	10 mL
Milk	3 cups	750 mL

(continued on next page)

Cook bacon in frying pan for 5 to 8 minutes. Drain. Add onion. Sauté until onion is soft.

Cook potato in water in large saucepan until tender. Do not drain.

Add remaining 5 ingredients. Add bacon and onion. Stir. Heat through. Makes 8¾ cups (2.1 L). Serves 8.

1 serving: 167 Calories; 3.5 g Total Fat; 590 mg Sodium; 7 g Protein; 30 g Carbohydrate; 2 g Dietary Fiber

VEGETABLE CREAM SOUP

A thick creamy soup with tiny bits of green showing through. Yum!

Chopped onion	½ cup	125 mL
Diced carrot	1 cup	250 mL
Frozen green beans	⅔ cup	150 mL
Frozen kernel corn	½ cup	125 mL
Diced parsnip (or yellow turnip)	1 cup	250 mL
Water	1 cup	250 mL
Frozen peas	½ cup	125 mL
Celery salt	⅛ tsp.	0.5 mL
Salt	½ tsp.	2 mL
Pepper	⅛ tsp.	0.5 mL
Chicken bouillon powder	2 tsp.	10 mL
Milk	2 cups	500 mL

Place first 6 ingredients in medium saucepan. Bring to a boil. Cover. Simmer until vegetables are cooked. Transfer to blender, including any liquid left in saucepan.

Add peas, celery salt, salt, pepper and bouillon powder. Process until smooth. Pour back into saucepan. Heat, stirring often, until simmering. Simmer for 1 minute.

Add milk. Heat, stirring often, until almost boiling. Makes 5 cups (1.25 L). Serves 4.

1 serving: 147 Calories; 2.1 g Total Fat; 807 mg Sodium; 8 g Protein; 26 g Carbohydrate; 4 g Dietary Fiber

Paré Pointer

When a bee is on a bluebell you have a humdinger.

GOUDA SOUP

A thick chowder texture. A small serving is sufficient.

Skim evaporated milk	13½ oz.	385 mL
All-purpose flour	¼ cup	60 mL
Milk	2 cups	500 mL
Salt	½ tsp.	2 mL
Pepper (white is best), sprinkle		
Worcestershire sauce	¾ tsp.	4 mL
Grated Gouda (or Edam) cheese	2 cups	500 mL
Dried chopped chives, for garnish	2 tbsp.	30 mL
Grated Gouda (or Edam) cheese, for garnish	2 tbsp.	30 mL

Whisk evaporated milk into flour in large saucepan until no lumps remain.

Add next 4 ingredients. Heat, stirring continually, until boiling and slightly thickened.

Add first amount of cheese. Whisk until melted.

Sprinkle each bowl of soup with chives and second amount of cheese. Serve very hot. Makes 4½ cups (1.1 L). Serves 6.

1 serving: *256 Calories; 12.3 g Total Fat; 692 mg Sodium; 19 g Protein; 17 g Carbohydrate; trace Dietary Fiber*

1. Prize Mushrooms, page 80
2. Picture Book Salad, page 135
3. Peach Soup, page 147
4. Shrimp Papaya Salad, page 130

PURÉED BEAN SOUP

Vary the color by varying the beans. Serve with a dollop of sour cream or yogurt. Good soup.

Hard margarine (or butter)	2 tsp.	10 mL
Finely chopped onion	¼ cup	60 mL
Grated carrot	½ cup	125 mL
Garlic clove, minced (or ¼ tsp., 1 mL, garlic powder)	1	1
Water	2½ cups	625 mL
Chicken bouillon powder	1 tbsp.	15 mL
Canned lima beans, drained	14 oz.	398 mL
Sherry (or alcohol-free sherry)	1 tbsp.	15 mL

Heat margarine in large saucepan. Add onion, carrot and garlic. Sauté until onion is soft.

Add water and bouillon powder. Simmer for 15 minutes.

Add beans. Simmer for 15 minutes. Process in blender until puréed. Return to saucepan. Heat through.

Stir in sherry. Makes 3 cups (750 mL). Serves 4.

1 serving: *107 Calories; 2.6 g Total Fat; 658 mg Sodium; 5 g Protein; 16 g Carbohydrate; 1 g Dietary Fiber*

Variation: Substitute a 19 oz. (540 mL) can of drained black beans for the lima beans. Soup will be darker in color.

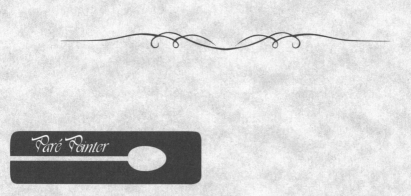

Paré Pointer

When a goat eats a dictionary you can take the words right out of his mouth.

CREAM OF SHRIMP SOUP

Simply doctor a can of soup to get this end result.

Hard margarine (or butter)	2 tsp.	10 mL
Chopped celery	3 tbsp.	50 mL
Green onions, chopped	3	3
Condensed cream of asparagus soup	2 x 10 oz.	2 x 284 mL
Milk	1½ cups	375 mL
Garlic powder	¼ tsp.	1 mL
Worcestershire sauce	1 tsp.	5 mL
Cayenne pepper	1/16 tsp.	0.5 mL
Skim evaporated milk	½ cup	125 mL
Cooked small fresh (or frozen, thawed) shrimp	½ lb.	225 g
Salt	½ tsp.	2 mL
Pepper	¼ tsp.	1 mL
Sherry (or alcohol-free sherry or white wine)	1 tbsp.	15 mL

Melt margarine in large saucepan. Add celery and green onion. Sauté until celery has softened a bit.

Add next 6 ingredients. Stir together well. Bring to a boil.

Add remaining 4 ingredients. Return just to a boil. Serve immediately. Makes 5½ cups (1.4 L). Serves 6.

1 serving: *167 Calories; 5.7 g Total Fat; 1183 mg Sodium; 14 g Protein; 15 g Carbohydrate; trace Dietary Fiber*

BEEF WINE CONSOMMÉ

A clear rich rusty brown color. Easy to double.

Water	3 cups	750 mL
Onion slivers	1 tbsp.	15 mL
Carrot slivers	1 tbsp.	15 mL
Celery slivers	1 tbsp.	15 mL
Yellow turnip (or parsnip) slivers	1 tbsp.	15 mL
Chopped green onion	1 tbsp.	15 mL
Beef bouillon powder	1 tbsp.	15 mL
Granulated sugar	1½ tsp.	7 mL
Lemon juice	½ tsp.	2 mL
Salt	¼ tsp.	1 mL
Red (or alcohol-free red) wine	¼ cup	60 mL

(continued on next page)

Place first 6 ingredients in medium saucepan. Bring to a boil. Cover. Simmer for about 5 minutes until vegetables are cooked.

Add remaining 5 ingredients. Stir. Simmer for about 1 minute. Makes 3 cups (750 mL). Serves 4.

1 serving: 28 Calories; 0.3 g Total Fat; 619 mg Sodium; 1 g Protein; 4 g Carbohydrate; trace Dietary Fiber

PEACH SOUP

Bright cheery-looking chilled soup.

Hard margarine (or butter)	1 tbsp.	15 mL
Small onion, chopped	1	1
Granulated sugar	1½ tbsp.	25 mL
Curry powder	½ tsp.	2 mL
Turmeric	⅛ tsp.	0.5 mL
Chili powder, just a pinch		
Citric acid (available at drug store)	½ tsp.	2 mL
Salt	⅛ tsp.	0.5 mL
All-purpose flour	1 tbsp.	15 mL
Canned sliced peaches, with juice	14 oz.	398 mL
Water	2 cups	500 mL
Lemon juice	1 tsp.	5 mL
Cooking apples (McIntosh is good), peeled and chopped	2	2
Skim evaporated milk (or light cream)	⅓ cup	75 mL

Heat margarine in medium saucepan. Add onion, sugar, spices, citric acid and salt. Sauté until onion is soft.

Mix in flour.

Add peaches with juice, water, lemon juice and apple. Sauté until apple is cooked. Transfer to blender. Process until smooth.

Stir in evaporated milk. Chill. Makes 5⅓ cups (1.25 L). Serves 6.

1 serving: 107 Calories; 2.2 g Total Fat; 102 mg Sodium; 2 g Protein; 22 g Carbohydrate; 2 g Dietary Fiber

Pictured on page 143.

PUMPKIN SOUP

Golden orange with a thick texture. Make your own design with the sour cream garnish.

Skim evaporated milk	13½ oz.	385 mL
Canned pumpkin (without added spices)	14 oz.	398 mL
Milk	½ cup	125 mL
Salt	¾ tsp.	4 mL
Ground nutmeg	1/16 tsp.	0.5 mL
Maple (or maple-flavored) syrup	1½ tbsp.	25 mL
Sour cream, for garnish (optional)		

Combine first 5 ingredients in large saucepan. Stir. Heat, stirring often, until almost boiling. Remove from heat.

Stir in maple syrup. Divide among 4 bowls.

Add swirl of sour cream to each. Makes scant 4 cups (1 L). Serves 4.

1 serving: 150 Calories; 0.9 g Total Fat; 651 mg Sodium; 10 g Protein; 27 g Carbohydrate; 2 g Dietary Fiber

ALMOND SOUP

An interesting texture. Serve hot or chilled.

Condensed chicken broth	2 × 10 oz.	2 × 284 mL
Ground blanched almonds	3½ oz.	100 g
Small bay leaf	1	1
Milk	1 cup	250 mL
All-purpose flour	2 tbsp.	30 mL
Hard margarine (or butter)	2 tsp.	10 mL
Skim evaporated milk (or light cream)	1 cup	250 mL
Lemon pepper	⅛ tsp.	0.5 mL
Chopped sliced almonds, toasted in 350°F (175°C) oven for 5 to 10 minutes	1 tbsp.	15 mL

(continued on next page)

Heat first 3 ingredients in medium saucepan until simmering. Cover. Simmer for 20 minutes. Discard bay leaf.

Whisk milk into flour in small bowl until smooth. Stir into simmering broth until boiling and thickened.

Stir in margarine, evaporated milk and lemon pepper. Heat through. Cool. Chill overnight for flavors to blend.

Serve chilled or hot. Sprinkle with toasted almonds just before serving. Makes 4 cups (1 L). Serves 6.

1 serving: *209 Calories; 12.2 g Total Fat; 719 mg Sodium; 13 g Protein; 13 g Carbohydrate; 1 g Dietary Fiber*

Variation: Stir in ¼ cup (60 mL) white wine just before serving.

LOBSTER BISQUE

Serve when price is no object. Recipe may be halved if desired. Rich flavor.

Condensed cream of mushroom soup	2 × 10 oz.	2 × 284 mL
Milk	2⅔ cups	650 mL
Skim evaporated milk	13½ oz.	385 mL
All-purpose flour	2 tbsp.	30 mL
Sherry (or alcohol-free sherry)	¼ cup	60 mL
Hot pepper sauce	¼ tsp.	1 mL
Chili sauce	¼ cup	60 mL
Canned frozen lobster meat, thawed (or imitation lobster), broken up	11.3 oz.	320 g

Paprika, sprinkle

Whisk first 7 ingredients in large saucepan until smooth. Heat, stirring occasionally, until almost boiling.

Add lobster meat. Stir. Process in blender to purée if desired. Return to saucepan. Heat through.

Sprinkle with paprika to serve. Makes 8 cups (2 L). Serves 12.

1 serving: *144 Calories; 4.7 g Total Fat; 658 mg Sodium; 11 g Protein; 13 g Carbohydrate; 1 g Dietary Fiber*

CRAB BISQUE: Omit lobster. Add canned crabmeat, drained and cartilage removed.

HOT AND SOUR SOUP

You may not have this uncommon vinegar on hand but if you have always wanted to try this soup, you may want to get some.

Condensed chicken broth	2 × 10 oz.	2 × 284 mL
Water	2 cups	500 mL
Tomato juice	10 oz.	284 mL
Rice (or white wine) vinegar	¼ cup	60 mL
Soy sauce	2 tbsp.	30 mL
Canned bamboo shoots, drained and cut julienne	8 oz.	227 mL
Chopped fresh mushrooms	½ cup	125 mL
Slivers red or yellow pepper, 1½ inches (3.8 cm) long	½ cup	125 mL
Hot pepper sauce	½ tsp.	2 mL
Dried crushed chilies	¼-½ tsp.	1-2 mL
Diagonally sliced green onion	¼ cup	60 mL
Cooked chicken (or ham or beef), cut julienne	½ cup	125 mL
Cornstarch	1½ tbsp.	25 mL
Water	¼ cup	60 mL
Large egg, fork-beaten	1	1

Combine first 10 ingredients in large saucepan. Bring to a boil. Simmer, uncovered, for 10 minutes.

Add green onion and chicken. Cook for 1 minute.

Stir cornstarch into water in small cup. Stir into soup until mixture is boiling and slightly thickened.

Slowly add beaten egg in a continuous stream while soup is boiling. Stir until threads form in the soup from the egg. Makes 7¾ cups (1.9 L). Serves 8.

1 serving: 71 Calories; 1.9 g Total Fat; 879 mg Sodium; 8 g Protein; 6 g Carbohydrate; 1 g Dietary Fiber

Pictured on page 125.

Throughout this book measurements are given in Conventional and Metric measure. To compensate for differences between the two measurements due to rounding, a full metric measure is not always used. The cup used is the standard 8 fluid ounce. Temperature is given in degrees Fahrenheit and Celsius. Baking pan measurements are in inches and centimetres as well as quarts and litres. An exact metric conversion is given below as well as the working equivalent (Standard Measure).

OVEN TEMPERATURES

Fahrenheit (°F)	Celsius (°C)
175°	80°
200°	95°
225°	110°
250°	120°
275°	140°
300°	150°
325°	160°
350°	175°
375°	190°
400°	205°
425°	220°
450°	230°
475°	240°
500°	260°

SPOONS

Conventional Measure	Metric Exact Conversion Millilitre (mL)	Metric Standard Measure Millilitre (mL)
1/8 teaspoon (tsp.)	0.6 mL	0.5 mL
1/4 teaspoon (tsp.)	1.2 mL	1 mL
1/2 teaspoon (tsp.)	2.4 mL	2 mL
1 teaspoon (tsp.)	4.7 mL	5 mL
2 teaspoons (tsp.)	9.4 mL	10 mL
1 tablespoon (tbsp.)	14.2 mL	15 mL

CUPS

	Metric Exact Conversion Millilitre (mL)	Metric Standard Measure Millilitre (mL)
1/4 cup (4 tbsp.)	56.8 mL	60 mL
1/3 cup (5 1/3 tbsp.)	75.6 mL	75 mL
1/2 cup (8 tbsp.)	113.7 mL	125 mL
2/3 cup (10 2/3 tbsp.)	151.2 mL	150 mL
3/4 cup (12 tbsp.)	170.5 mL	175 mL
1 cup (16 tbsp.)	227.3 mL	250 mL
4 1/2 cups	1022.9 mL	1000 mL (1 L)

PANS

Conventional Inches	Metric Centimetres
8x8 inch	20x20 cm
9x9 inch	22x22 cm
9x13 inch	22x33 cm
10x15 inch	25x38 cm
11x17 inch	28x43 cm
8x2 inch round	20x5 cm
9x2 inch round	22x5 cm
10x4 1/2 inch tube	25x11 cm
8x4x3 inch loaf	20x10x7.5 cm
9x5x3 inch loaf	22x12.5x7.5 cm

DRY MEASUREMENTS

Conventional Measure Ounces (oz.)	Metric Exact Conversion Grams (g)	Metric Standard Measure Grams (g)
1 oz.	28.3 g	28 g
2 oz.	56.7 g	57 g
3 oz.	85.0 g	85 g
4 oz.	113.4 g	125 g
5 oz.	141.7 g	140 g
6 oz.	170.1 g	170 g
7 oz.	198.4 g	200 g
8 oz.	226.8 g	250 g
16 oz.	453.6 g	500 g
32 oz.	907.2 g	1000 g (1 kg)

CASSEROLES (Canada & Britain)

Standard Size Casserole	Exact Metric Measure
1 qt. (5 cups)	1.13 L
1 1/2 qts. (7 1/2 cups)	1.69 L
2 qts. (10 cups)	2.25 L
2 1/2 qts. (12 1/2 cups)	2.81 L
3 qts. (15 cups)	3.38 L
4 qts. (20 cups)	4.5 L
5 qts. (25 cups)	5.63 L

CASSEROLES (United States)

Standard Size Casserole	Exact Metric Measure
1 qt. (4 cups)	900 mL
1 1/2 qts. (6 cups)	1.35 L
2 qts. (8 cups)	1.8 L
2 1/2 qts. (10 cups)	2.25 L
3 qts. (12 cups)	2.7 L
4 qts. (16 cups)	3.6 L
5 qts. (20 cups)	4.5 L

INDEX

STIR-FRY

Everyday recipes trusted by millions

Company's Coming

Chop, stir & serve.
Easy as 1, 2, 3!

Recipes for combining meats and vegetables.

- Beef
- Chicken
- Desserts
- Fish & Seafood
- Fruit
- Pork
- Salads
- Sandwiches
- Vegetables

Sample Recipe from STIR-FRY

SHRIMP CREOLE

To save time, use frozen mixed pepper strips if you can find them. Serve on a bed of hot rice.

Cooking oil	2 tsp.	10 mL
Small green pepper, cut into strips	½	½
Small red pepper, cut into strips	½	½
Small yellow pepper, cut into strips	½	½
Thinly sliced celery	⅓ cup	75 mL
Sliced onion	½ cup	125 mL
Frozen cooked medium shrimp	1 lb.	454 g
Canned diced tomatoes, drained and juice reserved	14 oz.	398 mL
Ketchup	1 tbsp.	15 mL
Chili powder	1 tsp.	5 mL
Brown sugar, packed	2 tsp.	10 mL
Salt	1 tsp.	5 mL
Cayenne pepper	⅛ tsp.	0.5 mL

Heat cooking oil in frying pan or wok until hot. Add pepper strips, celery and onion. Stir-fry for about 3 minutes.

Add shrimp. Stir-fry for 1 minute to heat.

Mix remaining 6 ingredients in small bowl. Add to shrimp mixture. Stir-fry until hot and sizzling. Makes 3 cups (750 mL), enough for 4 servings.

1 serving: 186 Calories; 4 g Total Fat; 1166 mg Sodium; 25 g Protein; 12 g Carbohydrate; 2 g Dietary Fiber

Company's Coming cookbooks are available at retail locations **throughout Canada!**

See mail order form

Buy any 2 cookbooks—choose a 3rd FREE of equal or less value than the lowest price paid.   *Available in French

Assorted Titles	CA$19.99 Canada	
CODE		
ML	Millennium Edition* (softcover) ◀NEW▶	US$19.99 USA & International
EE	Easy Entertaining* (hardcover)	US$19.99 USA & International
BE	Beef Today! (softcover)	US$15.99 USA & International

Lifestyle Series	CA$16.99 Canada			US$12.99 USA & International
CODE		**CODE**		**CODE**
LFC	Low-fat Cooking*	LFP	Low-fat Pasta*	GR	Grilling*◀NEW▶ (February 2000)

Kids Titles	CA$14.99 Canada		US$12.99 USA & International
CODE		**CODE**	
SN	Kids-Snacks*	KLU	Kids-Lunches

Original Series	CA$14.99 Canada			US$10.99 USA & International	
CODE		**CODE**		**CODE**	
SQ	150 Delicious Squares*	PA	Pasta*	KC	Kids Cooking*
CA	Casseroles*	CK	Cakes	FS	Fish & Seafood*
MU	Muffins & More*	BA	Barbecues*	BR	Breads*
SA	Salads*	DI	Dinners of the World	ME	Meatless Cooking*
AP	Appetizers	LU	Lunches*	CT	Cooking For Two*
DE	Desserts	PI	Pies*	BB	Breakfasts & Brunches*
SS	Soups & Sandwiches	LR	Light Recipes*	SC	Slow Cooker Recipes
HE	Holiday Entertaining*	MI	Microwave Cooking*	PZ	Pizza!*
CO	Cookies*	PR	Preserves*	ODM	One-Dish Meals*
VE	Vegetables	LCA	Light Casseroles*	ST	Starters*
MC	Main Courses	CH	Chicken, Etc.*	SF	Stir-Fry*◀NEW▶ (March 2000)

Greatest Hits	CA$12.99 Canada		US$9.99 USA & International
CODE		**CODE**	
BML	Biscuits, Muffins & Loaves*	SAS	Soups & Salads* ◀NEW▶ April 2000
DSD	Dips, Spreads & Dressings*	SAW	Sandwiches & Wraps* ◀NEW▶ April 2000

Select Series	CA$10.99 Canada			US$7.99 USA & International
CODE		**CODE**		**CODE**
GB	Ground Beef*	S&M	Sauces & Marinades*	MAS	Make-Ahead Salads
B&R	Beans & Rice*	TMM	30-Minute Meals*	NBD	No-Bake Desserts

Company's Coming
COOKBOOKS®

www.**companys**coming.com
visit our ↖web-site

COMPANY'S COMING PUBLISHING LIMITED
2311 - 96 Street
Edmonton, Alberta, Canada T6N 1G3
Tel: (780) 450-6223 Fax: (780) 450-1857

Mail Order Form

See facing page for list of cookbooks

QUANTITY	CODE	TITLE	PRICE EACH	PRICE TOTAL
			$	$
	TOTAL BOOKS (including FREE)			

DON'T FORGET to indicate your FREE book(s) (see exclusive mail order offer above) PLEASE PRINT

TOTAL BOOKS PURCHASED:

	INTERNATIONAL	CANADA & USA
Plus Shipping & Handling (PER DESTINATION)	$ 7.00 (one book)	$ 5.00 (1-3 books)
Additional Books (INCLUDING FREE BOOKS)	$ ($2.00 each)	$ ($1.00 each)
SUB-TOTAL	$	$
Canadian residents add G.S.T(7%)		$
TOTAL AMOUNT ENCLOSED	$	$

The Fine Print
- Orders outside Canada must be **PAID IN US FUNDS** by cheque or money order drawn on Canadian or US bank or by credit card.
- Make cheque or money order payable to: **COMPANY'S COMING PUBLISHING LIMITED**.
- Prices are expressed in Canadian dollars for Canada, US dollars for USA & International and are subject to change without prior notice.
- Orders are shipped surface mail. For courier rates, visit our web-site: **www.companyscoming.com** or contact us: **Tel: (780) 450-6223 Fax: (780) 450-1857**.
- Sorry, no C.O.D's.

☐ MasterCard ☐ VISA

_____ Expiry date

Account # _____

Name of cardholder _____

Cardholder's signature _____

Shipping Address
Send the cookbooks listed above to:

Name:

Street:

City: _____ Prov./State:

Country: _____ Postal Code/Zip:

Tel: ( )

E-mail address:

YES! **Please send a catalogue.**
☐ **English** ☐ **French**

Gift Giving
- Let us help you with your gift giving!
- We will send cookbooks directly to the recipients of your choice if you give us their names and addresses.
- Please specify the titles you wish to send to each person.
- If you would like to include your personal note or card, we will be pleased to enclose it with your gift order.
- Company's Coming Cookbooks make excellent gifts: Birthdays, bridal showers, Mother's Day, Father's Day, graduation or any occasion...collect them all!

COOKBOOKS

OVER
15 million
sold in series